Heinz A. Richter

The Conflicts of the Aegean in the 20th Century

PELEUS

STUDIEN ZUR

GESCHICHTE GRIECHENLANDS UND ZYPERNS

HERAUSGEGEBEN VON HEINZ A. RICHTER

BAND 113

HARRASSOWITZ VERLAG WIESBADEN
IN KOMMISSION

VORMALS VERLAG FRANZ PHILIPP RUTZEN
WWW.RUTZEN-VERLAG.DE

Heinz A. Richter

The Conflicts of the Aegean in the 20th Century

Translated and modified edition

2021

HARRASSOWITZ VERLAG • WIESBADEN
IN KOMMISSION

PELEUS
Studien zur Archäologie und Geschichte Griechenlands und Zyperns
Herausgegeben von Heinz A. Richter
Band 113

Umschlagvignetten:
Umschlagbild: Turkish map showing demands in the Aegean
Gegenüber Titelblatt: Innenbild einer Schale des Peithinosmalers, Berlin, Pergamonmuseum (CVA Berlin 2, Taf. 61).

Bibliografische Information der Deutschen Nationalbibliothek
Die Deutsche Nationalbibliothek verzeichnet diese Publikation in der Deutschen Nationalbibliografie; detaillierte bibliografische Daten sind im Internet über https://dnb.de/ abrufbar.

Bibliographic information published by the Deutsche Nationalbibliothek
The Deutsche Nationalbibliothek lists this publication in the Deutsche Nationalbibliografie; detailed bibliographic data are available in the internet at https://dnb.de/

Printed in Germany on fade resistant and archival quality paper (PH 7 neutral).
Gesamtherstellung: Beltz Bad Langensalza GmbH, Bad Langensalza

www.harrassowitz-verlag.de

ISBN 978-3-447-11761-8
ISSN 1868-1476

Content

I dedicate this study to Eleni and Volker
who continously helped me
solving computer problems

FOREWORD

The present work originated from a study written for the Federal Institute for Eastern European and International Studies. The aim of the work at that time was to give the reader an overview of the historical genesis of the Greek-Turkish conflict and its development up to 1986. At the same time, an attempt was made to place the conflict in the context of international politics.

The changes in world politics over the past two years have also had an impact on this conflict: entrenched positions began to move and the crisis of March 1987 accelerated this development. In January 1988, the prime ministers of Greece and Turkey, Papandreou and Özal, initiated the process that has since borne the name of Davos through their talks in the Swiss resort town. The Greek-Turkish dialogue had begun. This process has not yet achieved a decisive breakthrough, but both sides agree that the use of force should be ruled out to solve the problems existing between them. This dynamic development was so fascinating that it even became a topic for the German media. However, the portrayals were mostly not very differentiated and confined to the development in Cyprus. It therefore seemed sensible to update the above-mentioned study. At the same time, the study itself was revised and important aspects were added. In particular, important documents were included that are often difficult to access, but which make it easier for the reader to make his or her own judgements.

This study was first published in German in 1989[1]. Several years ago it went out of print and readers wanting to inform themselves on the topics described in this study do no longer have a chance to do so. Thus I decided to republish this study but this time in English.

When I translated the text I discovered that almost none of the facts changed since the 1980ies. Facts, which I had described and analysed then had not changed in the 40 years which have passed since. The conflicts continue to exist and some new ones were added. A basic alteration is found in the change of leadership in Turkey which follows a completely different policy than its predecessors.

Forty years ago the leaders in Ankara and Athens were in mutual contact and there were positive results based on these contacts.

As regards Turkish policy towards Cyprus there was a fundamental change. A few years ago Ankara announced that the North of Cyprus would be annexed. If this did not happen then this was due to the resistance of the Turkish Cypriots under the leaderdhip of Mustafa Akinci. Ankara gave up but recently it announced that it was intended to annex the hotel town of Varosha which was uninhabited and did not belong to neither of the two states in Cyprus. Obviously the leader in Ankara expected no resistance if the empty town was annexed. But international protests prevented this undertaking. Therefore nothing changed in Cyprus.

But the Aegean conflict was enriched by the Arab refugees who appeared in Turkey after the conflict in Syria and Iraq. When too many refugees arrived many were transported to the Greek islands near the Turkish coast.When no more refugees could be brought there the EU paid some financial help to Turkey so that they might remain in Turkey. When too many refugees arrived the Turkish leader decided to send some to Europe directly but they were stopped by the Greeks at the Evros frontier. Thus this problem remains.

However this problem was enlarged when gas was found on the Cypriot shelf and Ankara

1 Heinz A. Richter, *Friede in der Ägäis? Zypern - Ägäis - Minderheiten* (Köln: Romiosini, 1989)

insisted that islands do not have shelves. But in this case European power companies have a say. And therefore this problem will be solved in favour of Cyprus.

Another problem are the Kurds but this is an inner-Turkish matter. Recently more Kurds are pushed out of central Turkey to the south east. But this problem does neither bother Cyprus nor Europe. It is a problem Ankara itself must solve.

Thus we can see that despite some of the old problems have vanished there are enough new ones to keep Turkey in trouble, and lastly cause Europe headaches.

THE GREEK-TURKISH CONFLICT UNTIL 1988

Introduction

The current conflict in the Aegean is both ancient and highly topical. Ultimately, it is about the question: who controls the two mainland coasts and the island bridge connecting them in the Aegean. The stages of this conflict range from the battle for Troy to the Persian Wars (490 and 480 B.C.), the conquest of Constantinople (1453) and the so-called Asia Minor catastrophe in 1922. While the historical significance of the first two historical events is clear to every Western European, knowledge of cle subsequent developments in the Aegean region during the approximately 400 years of Ottoman occupation is extremely limited.

The 400-year Ottoman occupation shaped the relationship between Turks and Greeks, and the liberation struggle, which lasted about 100 years and was waged by both sides, sometimes with the most brutal means, created the image on the Greek side of a hereditary enemy to be wary of.

This fear was reinforced by a collective sense of time that was completely different from that of Western Europe: the fall of Constantinople was hardly history, the Ottoman occupation was the day before yesterday and the liberation struggle ended only yesterday; the Greek expansion attempt in 1921 and 1922, which ended with the so-called Asia Minor catastrophe, the expulsion of the Greeks from Asia Minor, is still the living present.

Although the main points of conflict were resolved in the 1923 Treaty of Lausanne; the border issue was settled[2] and the minorities in Macedonia and Asia Minor were largely exchanged, so that at first glance there were actually no longer any areas of friction, traumas and sensitivities remained that could not be overcome in the following short reconciliation phase under Eleftherios Venizelos and Atatürk until 1935. The presence of about 1.5 million Asia Minor refugees among a population of about 6 million at that time (the German comparative figures after 1945 are: Refugees approx. 5 million, population approx. 60 million) and the problem of their integration (without West German economic miracle), which lasted until after the Second World War, formed a constant element of memory until recent times. Added to this were Turkish actions that kept mistrust alive. On the one hand, Turkey provided humanitarian aid to the neighbouring country during the horrific famine winter of the first year of occupation, 1941 to 1942, through food deliveries financed mainly by expatriate Greeks, and assisted Greek refugees on their way to Egypt, but on the other hand, it took massive action against Istanbul's economically prosperous Greek minority, which was thereby brought to the brink of ruin, a fact overlooked in the turmoil of the Second World War.[3]

In 1947, both countries became recipients of American aid under the Truman Doctrine, and in the early 1950s, both joined NATO. Traditional adversaries had become allies. The idea that allies could get into a serious conflict that would bring them to the brink of war several times seemed absurd, since Franco-German cooperation had proven that it was possible to

---

1 The most interesting provision in our context is found in Article 16 of the Treaty of Lausanne: "Turkey declares that it renounces all rights and titles, of any nature. concerning the territories situated beyond the boundaries provided for by the present Treaty as weil as the islands (except those the sovereignty of which are recognised to her by the same Treaty). while the future of the said territories and islands has been or will be settled by the interested parties, The provisions of the present Article do not prejudice the particular arrangements agreed to or to be agreed between Turkey and ist neighbouring countries on account of this vicinity." Quoted after *The Status Quo in the Aegean.* Edited by Institute for Political Studies. (Athen, no date), p. 16.

2 Emmanouil Tsouderos, *Diplomatika paraskinia* 1941 -1944 (Athen. Aetos, 1950), p. 203f. Tsouderos was prime minister of the Greek government-in-exile from 1941 to 1944. The memoirs of one of those involved at the time provide information about the capital tax policy of those years, which hit the minorities living in Turkey the hardest: Fail\ Ökte, *The Tragedy of the Turkish Capital Tax* (London: Croom Helm, 1987).

overcome hereditary enmity. But exactly the unimaginable happened: In the mid-1950s, the Cyprus conflict flared up, into which both NATO countries were immediately drawn, and in the mid-1970s, the direct confrontation of Greece and Turkey in the Aegean followed. Since both centres of conflict influence each other and form only partial aspects of the larger Greek-Turkish conflict, the following analysis must always keep both centres of conflict in mind. At the same time, the international impact of this conflict on NATO and the reactions of the Soviet Union will be observed.

The potential for conflict

Before presenting the chronological genesis of the conflict and military data, in order to be able to better assess the conflict potential. The figures should, however, be taken with some caution as approximate comparative values. The statistics of the countries are not too reliable.

According to the census of 1981, Greece had a population of 9.7 million, i.e. 74 inhabitants per square kilometre. Of these, 65 percent lived in cities and 23 percent were under 15 years old. (Comparative figures for Germany: 248 inhabitants per square kilometre, 92 per cent urban, 19.9 per cent under 15). The Greek population grew by an average of slightly less than 1 per cent per annum over the last 30 years (1980: 0.7 per cent). The illiteracy rate was 36 per cent in 1985.[1]

Turkey had 46.3 million inhabitants in 1982 (1978 census), i.e. 55 inhabitants per square kilometre. 44 per cent of the population was urban and 40 per cent was younger than 1 5 years. The Turkish population increased on average by about 2.5 per cent per annum over the last 30 years (1976-79: 2.07 per cent). The illiteracy rate was 38 per cent.

Projected to the end of the century, this means that there will be about 11.5 million Greeks and about 72 million Turks in the year 2000, provided that the reproductive behaviour of the population does not change significantly. The per capita income of the Greeks in 1981 was US $ 4,420 (1979: $ 3,890). The gross national product of Greece reached US $ 42,890 million in the same year (1979: $ 36,710 million). The per capita income of the Turks in the same year was $1,540 (1979: $1,330) and the gross national product was $70,210 million (1979: $58,760 million). Greece's inflation rate in 1982 and 1983 was 20 per cent, Turkey's 41 and 30 per cent respectively. The national debt in 1982 was $10.6 billion, that of Turkey $22.3 billion.

Of the 4.1 million employed persons in Greece in 1982, 35.7 percent worked in agriculture and 30.2 percent in industry. The comparable figures for Turkey are 19.5 million workers, of whom 51.5 per cent were in agriculture and 16.5 per cent in industry. Greece's energy consumption in 1979 was 19,458 GWh, Turkey's was about 4 times lower, although Greece even exports electricity. Vehicle density in 1980 was just over 50 cars per 1,000 inhabitants in Greece and 11 cars in Turkey. The Greek merchant fleet in 1980 was 39.5 million GRT (the largest fleet in Europe), while Turkey's was 1.2 million GRT. The largest asset of Greek foreign trade is tourism, which brought in US$ 21,556 million in 19821. Turkey's largest source of foreign exchange is the remittances of guest workers, which amounted to about US$ 2.1 billion in 1982.[2]

The Greek armed forces had a total strength of 187,000 men in 1984, of which 137,000 were conscripts and 1,800 women. The Turkish armed forces totalled 602,000 in 1984, of which 544,000 were conscripts. Greece's defence expenditure in 1983 was about US$ 1.7 billion, Turkey's US$ 1.9 billion. Foreign military aid to Greece amounted to US$ 280 million in

---

1 *Athens News Agency*, 9.September 1986.

2 *Dierke Weltstatistik 1985/1986.* (München: DTV, 1986), p. 64f and 90f; as well as European Community, *Die Europäische Gemeinschaft und der Mittelmeerraum,* (Luxemburg, 1985).

1983, that to Turkey to about US$ 460 million. Most of the weapons of both armed forces come from aid deliveries by the USA and its allies and are outdated, in some cases even obsolete. While Turkey, due to a lack of foreign currency, is only in a limited position to purchase weapons on a larger scale from other sources and is therefore still dependent on military aid from the allies, Greece has modernised part of its arsenal in recent years by purchasing sophisticated French (AMX tanks) and American (F 116) weapons![1]

The numerical superiority of the Turkish armed forces is therefore likely to be at least partially offset by the higher quality of the Greek weapons. In addition, the Greek armed forces are far more likely to be able to integrate sophisticated technical equipment on a large scale due to the higher level of education of the population.

But any statement about the possible outcome of an armed clash between Greece and Turkey would be presumptuous and pure speculation. All of Greece's armed forces are under NATO control with the exception of the 1,750 troops stationed in Cyprus and the 450 officers and men seconded to the (Greek) Cypriot armed forces. Turkey has not subordinated its 4th Army, the so-called Aegean Army, which is heavily equipped with landing craft, to NATO, nor has the corps stationed on Cyprus with 2 infantry divisions (1 7,000), which is equipped with 150 tanks (M-47/48, M 113) and 21 2 pieces of artillery. But back to the actual topic. As was explained at the beginning, the Greek-Turkish conflict consists of several sub-conflicts: the Cyprus conflict, the conflict in the Aegean and the recently added conflict over Thrace. It seems sensible to treat the three conflicts according to their chronological occurrence. First, then, a look at the genesis of the Cyprus conflict.

The Cyprus Conflict until 1974

Since the emergence of the Greek nation state, there has been a steadily growing movement in Cyprus for unification (enosis) with the motherland under the leadership of the Orthodox Church. Until the Congress of Berlin (1878), these efforts were directed against the Ottoman Empire. In Berlin, however, the European powers conceded the occupation and administration of the island to Great Britain, although Cyprus remained tributary to Turkey. After Turkey entered the war on the side of the Central Powers in November 1914, Britain annexed Cyprus. In October 1915, the British government, Grey, offered Athens the cession of the island if Greece entered the war on the side of the Entente. However, the pro-German government of Constantine I refused. Two years later, however, when Venizelos led Greece into the war on the side of the Entente, this offer was not repeated.

When the population exchange between Greece and Turkey was agreed in Lausanne in 1923, there were considerations to carry it out in Cyprus as well. However, since the considerations remained, the Cypriots were spared the human tragedies of forced resettlement at the time, but the failure to carry out ethnic land consolidation created a political time bomb whose explosive force increased from year to year. Cyprus became a British crown colony in 1925. In 1931, the first violent demonstrations for annexation (enosis) to Greece took place, which were violently suppressed by the colonial power. The then Prime Minister Eleftherios Venizelos, whose country was similarly dependent on Great Britain, was forced to state: *"No matter how deep the response which the national wishes of the inhabitants of these islands (Venizelos also spoke about the then Italian Dodecanese islands) finds in the Greek soul, it is impossible for the Greek state to undertake support for their realisation, or to tolerate that its territories be used to organise a systematic reaction against the peace of these islands. Crucial and more*

1 *Yearbook of the International Institute for Strategic Studies.* (London, 1985).

than crucial interests of Greece impose the necessity of undisturbed friendship with Great Britain ... In fact we have the right to demand of the Greek inhabitants of these islands that they be less egotistical."[1]

Venizelos' course on the Enosis issue was essentially adhered to by all his successors in office until the 1950s. For Great Britain, on the other hand, giving up Cyprus was out of the question for strategic reasons, especially since the importance of Cyprus as an unsinkable aircraft carrier controlling the eastern Mediterranean had rather increased during the Second World War.[2] Accordingly, the British colonial power took no notice of an unofficial plebiscite organised in 1950 in which an overwhelming majority of Greek Cypriots voted for Enosis.[3] When the Cypriots then turned to Athens, they met with cool reluctance there. Athens did not want a dispute with London. The newly elected Archbishop of Cyprus Makarios brought movement into this deadlock. The archbishop, who was an ardent supporter of enosis, demanded that Athens take the Cyprus question to the UN, otherwise he would do so with the help of Arab states. Pressured in this way, Athens turned to London and offered the following: If London accepted the annexation of Cyprus to Greece, it could of course keep its existing military bases in Cyprus and get four additional ones in Greece itself. Foreign Minister Eden coolly rejected this offer: the British Empire was not for sale. There is no Cyprus question.[4]

When further attempts to solve the problem through bilateral negotiations between London and Athens also failed, and when Greek public opinion embraced the Enosis issue, Greek Prime Minister Papagos decided in 1954 to take the Cyprus problem to the UN himself. For London, however, a release of Cyprus into independence was out of the question. Foreign Minister Eden summed up the British position in the almost classic formula: *"In geography and tactical considerations, the Turks have the stronger claim on Cyprus; in race and language the Greeks; in strategy the British, as long as their industrial life depends on oil supplies from the Persian Gulf"*.[5] At the same time, Eden pointed out expressis verbis before the House of Commons that the Cyprus question was also a matter for Turkey.

But it was not only in Ankara that people reacted to Eden's statement. On 17 August 1954, the later Vice-President of the Republic of Cyprus, Dr. Fazil Kücük, published some programmatic thoughts in his newspaper *"Cyprus, let it be remembered, was, until 1878, apart of the Turkish Empire. In 1878 the island was ceded to Great Britain as a security against Russian threat. Great Britain took over Cyprus on the undertaking that she would hand her back to Turkey as soon as this threat was abated or receded...Nevertheless, having regard to the close association of the two countries [Britain and Turkeyl, the ever-increasing Soviet threat to*

---

1 Michael Attalides, *Gyprus. Nationalism and International Polities.* (Edinburg, 1979), p. 59f. *"Whatever echo the national aspirations of the inhabitants of these islands may evoke in the minds of the Greeks, it is impossible for the Greek state to do anything for their realisation or to allow the Greek territory to be used to organise systematic actions against the peace of these islands. Crucial, extremely important interests of Greece and the United Kingdom make it imperative to maintain undisturbed friendship with Great Britain ... We have indeed the right to demand that the Greek inhabitants of these islands be less selfish".*

2 When the then Greek Regent, Archbishop Damaskinos, visited London in September 1945, the then British Ambassador to Athens, Leeper, suggested that Cyprus should be ceded to Greece after all. Foreign Secretary Bevin and the Foreign Office were in favour, the Golonial Office and the General Staff were against and prevailed.

3 Out of 24,700 votes cast, 21,000 were in favour of Enosis. Ludwig Dischler, *Die Zypernfrage* (Frankfurt: Metzner, 1960), p. 28.

4 Francois Grouzet, *Le conflit de Chypre* 1946-1959. Volume I. (Brussels, 1973), p. 56.

5 Anthony Eden, *Full Circle.* (london, 1960), p. 315.
"From a geographical and tactical point of view, the Turks have the greater claim to Cyprus; from a racial and linguistic point of view, the Greeks; from a strategic point of view, the British, as long as their industry depends on oil supplies from the Persian Gulf".

humanity and world security and the moral side of the question, it should be abundantly clear to all intelligent men that Great Britain cannot consider the handing over of the government to any nation except with the full consent and approval of its former owner -Turkey ... But if Great Britain is going to consider this enosis question at all or is going to quit the island she has a legal as weil as a moral duty to call Turkey and hand Cyprus back to Turkey, and ask the Turkish government to deal with the enosis problem which the tolerant and iII-advised British administration has fostered in the island. From a legal as weil as moral point of view, Turkey ... has a first option to Cyprus...This has been the attitude of the Turkish government. .. The Turkish youth in Turkey, in fact, has grown up with the idea that as soon as Great Britain leaves the island the island will automatically be taken ·over by the Turks. It must be clear to all concerned that Turkey cannot tolerate seeing one of her former islands, Iying as it does only forty miles from her shores, handed over to a weak neighbour thousands [sic] of miles away, which is politically as weil as financially on the verge of bankruptcy".[1]

Britain's tactical manoeuvre to play Greece off against Turkey had serious consequences: From now on, Turkey would be involved in all issues concerning Cyprus. At the same time, the two future conflict hotspots in the Aegean and in Thrace were looming on the horizon. Since no one objected to Turkey's more far-reaching demands - apparently no one took them seriously - Ankara interpreted this as a kind of consent and made them longer-term objectives of Turkish foreign policy that would be translated into reality when the opportunity arose. At the same time, a kind of Turkish expansionist roadmap had been launched: Cyprus, Aegean, Thrace. An anti-colonialist struggle became an international flashpoint that could not be defused until the present.[2]

But it was not only the British who were against Athens' undertaking to bring the Cyprus question before the UN, but also the USA. Secretary of State Dulles considered the project harmful to US security interests in the Middle East and fatal to the recently concluded Balkan pact between Belgrade, Athens and Ankara. At the UN debate, therefore, the Anglo-Americans let the Greek proposal slip through their fingers.[3]

Encouraged by the successful anti-colonialist struggle in other countries, the first guerrilla actions of the EOKA (Ethniki Organosi Kyprion Agoniston National Organisation of Cypriot

---

1 Ludwig Dischler, a. a. *0.*, p. 31.

2 Quoted after Christopher Hitchens, *Cyprus* (London: Quartet Books, 1984), p. 41 f. In 1955 when the British banned all Greek Cypriot parties, they allowed Dr. Kücük to found a new party, which bore the remarkable name "Cyprus is Turkish Party".. *ibidem,* p. 45.
Cyprus, as we know, was part of the Turkish Empire until 1878. In 1878, the island was ceded to Britain as a protective measure against the Russian threat. Britain took over Cyprus with the assurance that it would return the island to Turkey as soon as this threat abated or disappeared ... Considering the close relations between Britain and Turkey, the ever-increasing Soviet threat to humanity and world security, and the moral side of the question, it should be clear as a bell to all intelligent people that Britain cannot think of handing over the administration of the island to any other nation unless the former owner, Turkey, agrees to and approves it.... But if Britain wants to deal with the Enosis issue at all, or to leave the island, it has a legal as well as a moral duty to approach Turkey, to return Cyprus to it, and to ask the Turkish government to deal with the Enosis problem, which the tolerant but ill-advised British administration has raised on the island. From the legal as well as moral point of view, Turkey has the first option on Cyprus ... This has long been the position of the Turkish government ... Young people in Turkey have grown up with the idea that as soon as Britain leaves the island, Enosis will automatically be taken over by Turkey. It must be clear to all concerned that Turkey cannot tolerate one of its former islands, only 40 miles off its coast, being handed over to a weak neighbour thousands of miles away and politically and financially on the brink of bankruptcy.

3 Van Coufoudakis, "United States Foreign Policy", in: *US Foreign Policy toward Greece and Cyprus. The Clash of Principle and Pragmatism.* Edited by Theodore A. Couloumbis &. Sallie M. Hicks.(Washington, 1975), p. 106f.

Fighters) then began on 1 April 1955 under the leadership of the right-wing extremist Giorgios Grivas[1] against the British, which escalated into a general uprising by summer 1955. London responded by inviting Greece and Turkey to a conference on possible self-government for Cyprus, thus officially bringing Turkey into play as an equal partner for the first time.

Even before the conference, Eden had encouraged Ankara to steer a hard course and make it clear to Athens that Ankara was not prepared to hand over Cyprus to the Greeks.[2] When the conference reached an impasse, an event with far-reaching consequences occurred: A Turkish agent provocateur carried out a bomb attack on the Turkish Consulate General in Thessaloniki and on the house where Atatürk was born. The very next day, the Turkish people's anger "reacted": In Istanbul and other Turkish cities, there were riots against the Greek minority. Both actions were demonstrably organised by Menderes' government.[3] Menderes' reckless action had serious consequences, because it renewed the Turkish-Greek conflict and linked it to the conflict over Cyprus. From then on, the two conflicts formed a single entity.

The development of the next three years is so complicated that this study does not include a detailed description. Only a few partial aspects relevant to the further development should be elaborated. The EOKA was fundamentally different from all liberation movements of that time. The majority of its members were patriots who wanted to end colonial rule and join the motherland. But a part of its leadership around Grivas at the same time represented a militant anti-communism and chauvinist "Hellenism", which ruled out cooperation with the Cypriot communists and the Turkish Cypriots. This neutralised the only force, AKEL, which organisationally and programmatically would have been able to bridge the latent ethnic divide, e.g. through its trade union PEO (Pankypria Ergatiki Omospondia '" Pan-Cypriot Workers' Federation)[4] Grivas knew three enemies: the British, the communists and the Turkish Cypriots,[5] although at times he was not clear whether he should give priority to the British or the communists.

The British were well aware of Grivas's anti-communism and chauvinism and they exploited both: they tolerated his outrages against the communists, as this weakened AKEL and permanently weakened the cooperation of the ethnic groups at the trade union base, and they provoked him into anti-Turkish measures. However, they were less successful in the first endeavour, although they made a strong impact by banning AKEL: AKEL survived the double attacks. Their second plan, which was to split the two ethnic groups, was successfully realised.

To fight the EOKA, the British set up a special unit recruited almost entirely from members of the Turkish Cypriot minority. The deployment of this force soon provoked the first conflicts between the two ethnic groups. When Ankara then promoted the establishment of an underground organisation among the Turkish Cypriots Volkan, which was later renamed TMT (Türk Mudafa Teskilat '" Turkish Defence Organisation), which also fought the EOKA, the conflict escalated into an internal Cypriot civil war.

---

1 Giorgios Grivas was born in Cyprus in 1898. After attending the Athens Cadet School, he made a career in the Greek army. Towards the end of the occupation, he built up the anti-communist underground organisation Chi with the benevolent support of the German occupying power. After the Germans left, the British regarded Grivas' "troop" as a welcome Cypriot auxiliary force in the upcoming confrontation with the Party of Greek Resistance. In 1945, Chi became an instrument of terror for the extreme right. The conservative British author C. M. Woodhouse spoke of the Ku Klux Klan in this context. C. M. Woodhouse, *Apple of Discord. A Survey of Reeent Greek Politics in their International Setting* (London: Hutchinson, , 1981)

2 Niels Kadritzke/Wolf Wagner, *Im Fadenkreuz der Nato. Ermittlungen am Beispiel Cypern.* (Berlin: Rotbuch Verlag, 1976), p. 28.

3 Constantine Tsoucalas, *The Greek Tragedy.* (Harmondsworth:.Penquin, 1969), p. 159f.

4 Kadritzke, *a.a.O.,* p. 27.

5 Michael Attalides, Cyprus. Nationalism and International Politics (NewYork: St, Martin's Press, 1979), p. 48.

The TMT was as anti-communist and chauvinist as the EOKA, but not anti-British, and was therefore never banned by the British authorities throughout the struggle for independence. The TMT was a creation of the Menderes government and the Turkish General Staff. Its leaders were Turkish officers who were detached to Cyprus for this purpose. Their political advisor was a former official of the Colonial Administration, Rauf Denktash.[1] It is not entirely clear what Denktash's aims were at the time. However, it can be assumed with a high degree of probability that they hardly differed from those of the Turkish military, otherwise he would hardly have become a political advisor. In other words, Denktash was an acolyte of the Turkish military from the beginning of the conflict.

The TMT's first actions were against communist island Turks. Turkish Cypriot PEO trade unionists were terrorised. In 1958, the director of the Turkish office of the PEO, Ahmet Sadi, had to flee the country after an assassination attempt by the TMT. Other trade union leaders were murdered in the streets. Party and union offices were forced to close or were set on fire. Under massive threats, union members were forced to join the nationalist Turkish unions. Unlike the EOKA, the TMT was successful in its anti-communist campaign of destruction.

The TMT operated with similar "success" in its efforts to manoeuvre the two ethnic groups apart. In 1958, as Denktash admitted in a British television programme, agents provocateurs of the TMT organised a bomb attack on the Turkish Information Centre in Nicosia. In the riots provoked by this, the British forces of law and order looked the other way for some time before intervening. In the following months, the process of violence and counter-violence escalated to such an extent that one can speak of a civil war.

London watched the TMT's activities with sympathy, as the dispute confirmed British and Turkish claims that the two communities could not live together peacefully. At the same time, London encouraged Ankara to demand self-determination for its ethnic group, whereupon Ankara began a large-scale propaganda campaign for the division of the island (Turkish: Taksim) along the 35th parallel.

In the meantime, the conflict between the two ethnic groups on the island had created such tensions between the mother countries that they were on the brink of war several times. In the spring of 1955, Foreign Minister Zorlu openly threatened to attack Greece and invade Cyprus if the British gave up the island in favour of Greece. When, after the failed Suez adventure in 1956, the Macmillan government finally agreed to reduce its involvement in Cyprus, Ankara interpreted this as giving in on the Enosis issue and Menderes threatened to invade. This prompted the Americans to intervene. The result, after protracted negotiations between Ankara, Athens and London - the Cypriots did not take part in the negotiations - was the Zurich and London Agreements.[2]

The solution found in these treaties was a sham and ultimately only served to settle the conflict between the NATO allies. Formally, Cyprus became an independent republic. However, its sovereignty was suspended by the right of intervention of the three guarantor powers (GB, GR, TR), especially as they were even allowed to station troops on the island. As long as Greece and Turkey were in agreement, Cyprus was ultimately an indirect NATO member. But as soon as a new conflict broke out between the ethnic groups, from then on there was the immediate threat of a direct clash between Greece and Turkey.

---

1 Hitchens, *a.a.O.,* p. 116.

2 Kadritzke, a.a.O., p. 28f.

The Cyprus Constitution, which emerged from the Zurich and London Treaties, was doomed to failure from the outset because its premise - good neighbourly relations between the communities - no longer existed. Its basic principle was a kind of ethnic taksim of the three constitutional powers, which institutionalised the ethnic division and prevented a rapprochement of the ethnic groups. The crucial design flaw of the constitution, however, was the absolute veto power of the Turkish minority. Cyprus became the first state whose constitution explicitly forbade the principle of majority rule. Without a change in the constitution, Cyprus would become ungovernable within a short time. Any attempt to change the constitution, however, would immediately bring the Turkish guarantor power on the scene and provoke a conflict between the mother countries.[1]

The dispute began in 1962, when Makarios, who had been elected president, tried to push through 13 amendments to the constitution in order to restart governance, which had been blocked by a Turkish Cypriot veto. When the Turkish Cypriot side categorically rejected any changes to the constitution, clashes between the ethnic groups broke out in 1963 and quickly escalated into civil war. With the two mother countries interfering in the conflict and the threat of a direct clash between Greece and Turkey in December 1963, the Americans intervened directly for the first time: President Johnson expressed his deep concern about the situation on the island to Makarios and the Turkish Vice-President of Cyprus, Kücük. Nevertheless, when rumours of an imminent armed intervention by Ankara increased, Makarios turned to the UN Security Council, which took note of the complaints but saw no reason to act [2]

Finally, at Makarios' request, the British guarantor power convened a conference of all parties for 15 January 1964 in London.

The conference failed after a short time because all parties stubbornly stuck to their demands: Ankara and the Turkish Cypriot representatives demanded' the partition of the island, Athens demanded Enosis, and the Cypriot government insisted on its independence. When Ankara again unleashed organised Turkish popular anger against Istanbul's Greek minority and war again threatened, London proposed a compromise: the British troops that had interposed themselves between the opposing parties in Nicosia at the end of 1963 as a kind of buffer should be reinforced by contingents from other NATO countries and form a peacekeeping force. The Cypriot government, however, rejected this proposal; if a peacekeeping force were to be sent, it would have to be under the direct control of the UN.

Nevertheless, London forwarded this proposal to Washington on 25 January. The Americans, for whom Makarios' course of neutrality had long been a thorn in the flesh, reacted positively. They wanted a pro-Western Cyprus to join Greece and Turkey in a solid anti-communist bloc and to join NATO. Therefore, on 28 January, they sent NATO commander Lemnitzer to Athens and Ankara. Ankara, which liked the NATO solution, 'readily accepted and shelved its intervention plans for the time being. The conservative interim government in Athens, which feared a Turkish intervention and was busy preparing for parliamentary elections, gave in to American pressure and accepted the NATO solution. An imposed solution to the Cyprus problem began to loom on the horizon. To prevent this, Makarios turned to the Russians. On 7 February, Nikita Khrushchev declared threateningly that the Soviet Union would come to the aid of the Republic of Cyprus against any foreign intervention. In the face

1 Tsoucalas, *op.cit,* p.162f.
2 *UN Yearbook* 1964. p. 150f

of this threat, the US reluctantly accepted the deployment of a UN peacekeeping force, the UNFICYP, after US Deputy Secretary of State George W.Ball made another futile attempt with Makarios himself on 12 February. Makarios' intransigent attitude and the intervention of the Soviet Union had ensured Cyprus' independence for the time being.[1]

In the next few months, the first UNFICYP units were sent to Cyprus, but the fighting continued. Ankara responded to the Cypriot government's pressure against the Turkish minority with repression against Istanbul's Greek minority. At the end of May, the situation came to a head again. Ankara resumed its preparations for intervention and Athens began to infiltrate regular Greek troops into Cyprus; in short, war between Greece and Turkey was again looming. That's when President Johnson intervened. In a rather rude letter to the Turkish Prime Minister Inönü, he warned him that the USA would not tolerate the use of weapons supplied by them to Turkey against Cyprus. Should Ankara nevertheless intervene in Cyprus and the Soviet Union react aggressively, NATO would not come to Turkey's aid.[2] Johnson then invited Inönü and the new Greek Prime Minister, Georgios Papandreou, to Washington for talks.

The talks with the Greeks began on 23 June 1964, with Johnson calling on Papandreou to hold a Greek-Turkish summit meeting with Inönü, who was still in the USA. Papandreou refused such a meeting without diplomatic preparation. Dean Rusk then put massive pressure on the Greeks: if the American proposal was not accepted, Turkey would attack Cyprus and/or Greece and America would not lift a finger. When Papandreou did not give in, the Americans proposed a meeting between representatives of Greece and Turkey in Geneva with Dean Acheson. When Papandreou objected that such a move would torpedo the UN's efforts, the Americans again threatened a Turkish attack. Papandreou, however, did not back down. Johnson therefore addressed another letter to Papandreou on 2 July, in which he ultimatively demanded that he come to an agreement with the Turks. At the same time, he made proposals for the partition and subsequent unification of Cyprus with Greece. Papandreou gave in[3] and on 4 July the talks began in Geneva, excluding the Cypriot government.

In Geneva, Johnson's special representative, Dean Acheson, presented the plan that went down in history under his name. Since this plan is still the basis of American Cyprus policy today and is therefore of fundamental importance, it will be examined in more detail.

Acheson stated that an independent state of Cyprus would threaten American interests. It could lead to Turkish intervention and, in such a case, make war between Greece and Turkey inevitable. He had loosened the ties of Greece and Turkey to the USA. He had strengthened the position of the CP of Cyprus (AKEL) and thus that of the Soviet Union in Cyprus. He had created a serious problem for the UN. And finally, he undermined NATO. The problem of Cyprus would only be solved for the USA when Cyprus ceased to exist as an independent state.

To solve the problem, Acheson made a startling proposal: the independence of Cyprus should be abolished by realising both Enosis and Taksim. The greater part of Cyprus should be annexed to Greece. The north-eastern peninsula of Karpasia should be ceded to Ankara as a military base. The Turkish Cypriots who did not want to emigrate to Turkey should be granted three autonomous cantons. Athens would have to undertake to protect the minority left

---

1 Kadritzke, *op.cit.* p. 45f. and Coufoudakis, *op.cit.*. p. 110f

2 The text of the letter can be found in: Cyprus, Public Information Office, ed., *Cyprus: The Problem in Perspective.* {Nicosia, 1969}, p. 36f sowie in Jacob M. Landau, "Johnson's 1964 Letter to Inönü and Greek Lobbying of the White House", in: *Jerusalem Papers on Peace Problems* {Jerusalem: The Leonard Davis Institute for International Relations. 1979}. pp. 19 -22; See alsoAli L. Karaosmanoglu, "Turkey's Security and the Middle East" *Foreign Affairs,* 62: 1, (19.83), p. 158.

3 Andreas Papandreou, *Democracy at Gunpoint: The Greek Front.* (NewYork, 1970), p. 134ff.

behind in accordance with the provisions of the Treaty of Lausanne, disarm all irregular forces, eliminate the influence of AKEL and stop the political activities of Makarios. Future disputes between the ethnic groups would be settled by the NATO Council.

However, the realisation of this plan should not be implemented through a formal agreement between Athens and Ankara, but by Athens simply declaring the annexation of the island to Greece. Through NATO mediation, the size of the Turkish share should then be discreetly determined. In any case, a public debate, especially in the Greek parliament, should be avoided.

When Papandreou, through the Greek ambassador in Washington, Alekos Matsas, indicated that no Greek parliament would accept such a plan, Johnson was more than blunt: *"Then listen to me... fuck your parliament and your Constitution. America is an elephant. Cyprus is a flea. Greece is a flea. If those two fleas continue itching the elephant, they may just get whacked by the elephant's trunk, whacked good."* When Ambassador Matsas objected that Greece was a democracy and the Greek Prime Minister could not act against the will of the Parliament, Johnson exploded: *"Let me tell you what answer I will give if I get that sort of reply back from your Prime Minister ... Who does he take himself for, anyway? I can't have a second de Gaulle on my hands. We pay a lot of good American dollars to the Greeks, Mr. Ambassador, If your Prime Minister gives me talk about Democracy, Parliament and Constitution, he, his Parliament and his Constitution may not last very long"*

All the while, Ankara's invasion preparations continued, so Papandreou turned to London for help, which only presented him with the Acheson plan in more diplomatic terms. When Papandreou continued to resist, the Americans contacted Makarios himself. When Makarios flatly refused to accept the American proposals, the Americans contacted Grivas, the former head of EOKA. Grivas had long regarded Makarios' course of neutrality as a betrayal: he was also a fanatical anti-communist who saw AKEL's existence as a provocation. He had returned to Cyprus in June, immediately taken over the command of the Cypriot National Guard and the infiltrated Greek units, and had begun to remove them from the influence of Makarios and Papandreou, with the approval of the Greek high command in Athens. Now, behind Makarios' back, he accepted the Acheson plan and promised to get Makarios out of the way.[1]

But since Makarios had Papandreou's support, the first step was to provoke a rift between the two. To this end, Grivas gave his forces the order to attack Turkish Cypriot positions near Kokkinia at the beginning of August. In retaliation, the Turkish air force bombed surrounding Greek Cypriot villages on 7 August and threatened some Greek islands in the East Aegean. When Makados saw that he could expect no help from Athens, he sent a request for military assistance to the Soviet Union, Egypt and Syria and brought the matter before the Security Council. At the same time, Makarios made it perfectly clear to Papandreou, who was wavering in the face of the acute danger of war, that the Acheson Plan, even in its recently modified form, could only be enforced on Cyprus by force of arms from Greece. Papandreou realised the impossibility of such a course of action and let the Geneva negotiations with Acheson collapse on 22 August.[2]

This took the Acheson plan off the table for the time being, but the power centre around Grivas, competing with the Cypriot government, continued to exist. When Papandreou tried

1 Christopher Hitchins, *Cyprus,* (London, Melbourne, New York 1984), p. *58t.*

2 Papandreou, *op.cit,* p. 137; Coutoudakis, *op.cit,* p. 115.

to get the connection between Grivas and the Greek high command under his control, this led to the infamous ASPIDA affair and finally to his fall.

The conservative Greek successor governments until the coup d'état of 21 April 1967 were more inclined to accommodate American wishes and therefore began secret negotiations with Turkey. In December 1966, an agreement was reached on the fringes of the NATO foreign ministers' meeting in Paris: the Greek and Turkish foreign ministers initialled a secret agreement, the main features of which corresponded to the Acheson Plan.[1] At the same time, the USA put Nicosia under pressure, for example by cutting off its economic aid to Cyprus in November 1966. Makarios responded by increasing his involvement in the Non-Aligned camp and strengthening Cyprus's relations with the socialist countries. In order to neutralise the threat posed by Grivas, he began to develop the Cypriot Gendarmerie instead of the National Guard, for which the CSSR later supplied him with weapons.

All the while, inter-ethnic differences continued to intensify. Ankara strengthened its control over the Turkish Cypriots and blocked efforts to find an intra-Cypriot settlement, as this would hinder the future division of the island. They were unintentionally supported by Makarios, who made the mistake of trying to persuade the Turkish minority to give in on the constitutional question through economic reprisals. He achieved the exact opposite: he drove the Turkish Cypriots into ever greater dependence on the motherland.

The military dictatorship in Greece naturally also had an impact on Cyprus. Dictator Papadopoulos made an amateurish attempt to reach a bilateral agreement with Demirel in September 1967, which failed miserably.[2] When in November 1967 Grivas once again provoked the Turks with a military action, Ankara ultimatively demanded the recall of Grivas and the withdrawal of all Greek troops (in divisional strength) illegally stationed on Cyprus since 1964. Since the Americans refused to back the Greek military junta - the risk of a new conflict so soon after the Arab-Israeli June War seemed too high - Athens had to comply with Ankara's demand. On Washington's instructions, however, the planned Turkish invasion of Cyprus did not take place. With the withdrawal of the illegal Greek forces, Athens lost face and at the same time the Greek position in Cyprus was decisively weakened, as was to become apparent in 1974.

In February 1968, presidential elections were held in Cyprus, from which Makarios emerged as a convincing winner. Obviously, the interest of the majority of Greek Cypriots in Enosis had cooled down considerably, as it would have brought the junta dictatorship to Cyprus as well.

After the election, Makarios initiated a new policy. The independence of Cyprus was to be secured by ending the internal strife. He initiated talks between the ethnic groups on a new constitution. In the following ,years, the two negotiators Kliridis and Denktash slowly made progress. Although there were always obstacles and tensions, overall there were signs that the artificially enforced division of 1958 was being overcome and that a compromise solution was being reached within Cyprus. In terms of foreign policy, Makarios secured this course through a policy of non-alignment.

Throughout this period, the Athens military junta tried by all means to undermine the Republic of Cyprus, not even shying away from assassination attempts against Makarios (e.g.

1 Kadritzke, *a.a.O.*, p. 52f.
2 Kadritzke, *a.a.O.*, p. 58; Hitchens, *a.a.O.*, p. 64f.

Hermes Plan March 1970). The subsequent investigation revealed that the assassination was orchestrated by the Greek secret service KYP, but that the CIA also had its fingers in the pie.[1]

In July 1970, Cyprus held parliamentary elections which produced two remarkable results: The pro-independence parties won a clear majority and the allied left emerged as the strongest force in the country. The election result was a clear rejection of the Athens junta's policy of annexation, and it alarmed the Americans. Vicious talk of Cyprus as the "Cuba of the Eastern Mediterranean" and of Makarios as a "Castro in a priest's skirt" did the rounds. Moreover, when Makarios visited the Soviet Union in June 1971, the Americans had had enough.

The State Department concluded that it could not be ruled out that Greece and Turkey would sooner or later agree on a double enosis. It would therefore serve American interests if Makarios or another Cypriot leader could be persuaded to accept such a solution. Encouraged in this way, the Greek junta foreign minister Panagiotis Pipinelis and his Turkish counterpart Ihsan Caglayangil decided on the fringes of the NATO meeting in Lisbon at the beginning of June 1971 to settle the conflict over Makarios' head, if necessary by force, with Ankara's representative urging swift action..[2]

The first thing Ankara did was to torpedo the inter-ethnic talks. In September, Athens sent Grivas to Cyprus again: to fight Makarios supporters and communists with the help of a new underground organisation (EOKA-B). Makarios recognised the danger and expanded the Cypriot gendarmerie as a counterweight to the Athens junta-controlled National Guard; the necessary weapons were supplied by the CSSR. A failed coup attempt by Grivas in 1972 and two more failed assassination attempts, again organised from Athens, poisoned the atmosphere beyond endurance. Massive terrorist attacks by the EOKA-B followed in 1973.

In October 1973, the Yom Kippur War broke out; it once again made the potential strategic importance of Cyprus for NATO and the USA abundantly clear. At the end of November 1973, a working seminar organised by the Americans took place in Rome, in which Kliridis and Denktash also participated. Here Cyrus Vance told the latter that the USA was not satisfied with the results of the intercommunal negotiations. Denktash promptly distanced himself from what had been achieved so far, and the new Turkish head of government, Ecevit, brought up a federation model. Vance also hinted that the USA would no longer prevent a Turkish invasion in the event of a new Cyprus crisis.[3]

In February 1974, Grivas died and the Athens KYP took over the leadership of the EOKA-B. On behalf of the new junta leader loannidis, Greek officers of the National Guard supplied the EOKA-B with weapons and at the same time prepared a coup against Makarios. When Makarios took countermeasures, thereby reducing the chances of a successful coup, loannidis let loose on 15 July 1974 in total ignorance of the real situation. But neither did the attempted assassination of Makarios succeed, nor did the putschists find a presentable collaborator as president. They therefore had to resort to a known psychopathic Turk-killer, Sampson, and appoint him president, which provoked Ankara to the utmost.[4]

Nevertheless, Ankara proceeded with deliberate caution, wanting to avoid another failure. On 16 July, Ecevit asked London to start consultations in accordance with the guarantee agreement. The British government agreed, and so Ecevit flew to London on 17 July. But Prime Minister Wilson and Foreign Secretary Callaghan were not inclined to honour their guarantee obligations. US Secretary of State Kissinger had given them to understand that they

---

1 Kadritzke, *op.cit,* p. 66f; Hitchens, *op-cit.,* p. 70.

2 Kadritzke, *op.cit,* p. 70f.

3 Kadritzke, *op.cit,* p. 70; Hitchens, *op.cit,* p. 72.

4 Kadritzke, *op.cit,* p. 73f.

should leave the matter to him. Accordingly, Deputy US Secretary of State Sisco, who had arrived in London shortly before, was brought in for the talks that evening. Ecevit quickly realised that the British government would do nothing and that Sisco had also come to the negotiations empty-handed. He rightly interpreted this as a green light for his plans.[1]

Even in his subsequent talks on 19 July in Athens and Ankara, Sisco did not seem to have urged either the junta or the Turks to give in or to show restraint. Thus assured, Ecevit gave the order to carry out the invasion of Cyprus that had been planned since the spring. On 20 July, Turkish troops landed in the north of Cyprus near Kyrenia and formed a bridgehead there.

In the meantime, the UN Security Council had dealt with the coup, and on 18 July Makarios himself had appeared in New York to bring charges against the coup plotters. When the news of the Turkish landing arrived in New York on 20 July, the Security Council immediately reconvened and called for a ceasefire. They accepted and on 22 July the ceasefire came into force.

On 23 July, the junta in Greece was overthrown. The next day, Karamanlis returned to Athens from his exile in Paris and formed a new democratic government. On 25 July, at British instigation, negotiations began between the Turkish Foreign Minister Günes and his Greek counterpart Mavros under the chairmanship of Callaghan. Nevertheless, Turkish troops expanded their bridgehead, and on 28 July Ecevit indicated in a press conference that a return to the status quo ante was out of the question. On 30 July, the three foreign ministers agreed that the current ceasefire line should be secured by UNFICYP units and that negotiations should continue on 8 August with the aim of establishing a stable peace with the participation of the Cypriots. At the same time, they pointed out that the Zurich and London Agreements were still in force.[2]

In the following days, however, Ankara reinforced its invasion forces so that they grew to 40,000 men and 200 tanks. At the same time, they continued to consolidate their bridgehead. On 8 August, as agreed, the second round of talks began in Geneva, but ended on 14 August, as both Günes and Denktash demanded the partition of the island, with the Turkish share of the territory of Cyprus being 34 per cent, despite Greek willingness to compromise .

Within two hours after the breakdown of negotiations, the Turkish forces went on the offensive. Immediately, British Foreign Secretary Callaghan approached the Security Council and the USA, offering the latter to place the British troops stationed on Cyprus under the command of UNFICYP in order to stop the Turkish advance, if necessary by force- Secretary of State Henry Kissinger waved this off. Despite a request by the Security Council on 14 August to stop the fighting, the Turkish forces continued their advance with all their might until 16 August, occupying about one third of Cyprus north of the so-called Attila Line from Lefka to Famagousta.

During its advance, the Turkish army, otherwise known for its discipline, deliberately terrorised the Greek Cypriots,[3] with the result that about a quarter of the Greek population, about 150,000 people, fled in panic to the south. This achieved the desired demographic change without exposing itself to accusations of forcible expulsion. This in turn led the National Guard and the EOKA-B to commit acts of terrorism against the Turkish minority in the south, who then fled to the north. The ethnic division of the island according to the Acheson Plan was complete. But the second part of the plan, the double enosis, the annexation of the

1 *Ibidem*, p. 78ff.

2 Hitchens, *op.cit,* p. 92f and Theodore A. Couloumbis, *The United States, Greece.. and Turkey. The Troubled Triangle.* (New York, 1983), p.89ff.

3 *Keesing/s Contemporary Archives*, p. 26 709.

two rump states to the respective motherland, failed for several reasons. Firstly, the legitimate head of state of Cyprus, Archbishop Makarios, had survived the coup and secondly, as already mentioned, the Athenian junta fell. Assuming Makarios' death, the double enosis could have been enforced as a fait accompli with loannidis through a cynical act of realpolitik. However, with the change to the democratic government of Karamanlis, this became impossible.[1]

But the new Greek government had made a serious mistake on 14 August: in protest against the passive attitude of the USA and NATO, Greece hastily withdrew from the military part of the NATO alliance on the grounds that, in the event of a conflict with Turkey, Greece must have full control over its armed forces. However, this meant that Athens lost any possibility of influencing the course of events, for example through the NATO Council.

Ankara, as mentioned, occupied Cyprus up to the Attila Line and turned a deaf ear to UN appeals. The northern part of Cyprus was under Turkish control. The significance of this occupation for the distribution of the population today may be illustrated by a few figures: in 1972, the total population of Cyprus was 645,000, of whom 503,000 were Greeks (78 per cent) and 116,000 Turks {18 per cent). In the now Turkish-occupied north, there were about 147,000 Greek Cypriots and about 64,000 Turkish Cypriots. In the south of Cyprus there were 355,000 Greeks and 51,000 Turks. Currently, there are about 110,000 Turkish Cypriots and less than 2,000 Greek Cypriots living in the north. The number of Turkish Cypriots in the south is probably less than 1,000; the remaining approx. 500,000 inhabitants are Greeks.

The expansion of the conflict after 1974

The hasty withdrawal from NATO on 14 August 1974 not only had serious consequences with regard to Cyprus, but it also inadvertently supported Ankara in its demands in the Aegean.

As mentioned above, in 1954 the Turkish delegate to the UN had declared that if the status of Cyprus changed, the Treaty of Lausanne and the balance it had achieved in the Aegean would be null and void. Ankara would then lay claim to the Greek East Aegean islands and to Western Thrace. Until 1973, however, this remained largely rhetoric. oil discoveries that year near the North Aegean island of Thasos, however, triggered the Aegean conflict.[2]

Before analysing the problem of the shelf and the question of the extent of territorial waters, it seems useful to first take a look at the relevant provisions of international law.

At the first UN Conference on the Law of the Sea in Geneva in 1958, the following was agreed on territorial waters: The territorial waters of a state, which had previously extended 6 nm into the sea, were henceforth to be 12 nm. In 1972, Greece ratified the Convention on the Law of the Sea - in contrast to Turkey - but waived its implementation. At present, Greece controls about 35 per cent of the Aegean waters, Turkey about 8.8 per cent. The share of international waters today is 56 per cent. If Greece and Turkey were to extend their territorial waters in the Aegean to 1 2 nm, the Greek share would increase to 63.9 per cent, but the Turkish share would only increase to 10 per cent. In this case, the international waters would decrease to 26 per cent, and the Aegean would become a Greek internal sea. As mentioned, Ankara did not ratify this Geneva Convention and very quickly gave Athens to understand that it would consider an expansion to 1 2 nm as casus belli. Greece then declared that it did not intend to extend, but that it reserved the right to do so. But Turkey, interestingly enough, extended its territorial waters in the Black Sea and off its southern coast to 1 2 nm.

1 *ibidem*, p.26.709.

2 C. D. Barkman. *Ambassadeur in Athene.* 1969 -1975 *van Dictatuur tot Demokratie.* {Gravenhage, 1984}, p. 160f. The English edition was published by Merlin Press London in 1988.

However, the Geneva Convention on the Law of the Sea also contained a number of provisions concerning the continental shelf. Article 1 (a) defined it as "the seabed and subsoil of submarine zones" lying off the coast of a state but outside territorial waters to a depth of 200 metres, or beyond that limit to a depth at which the overlying water column permits the exploitation of natural resources. Article 1 (b) grants the same to islands, i.e. each island has its own shelf.[1] Since the Aegean Sea outside Greek territorial waters only in very few places reaches a depth that prohibits exploitation of the seabed, the continental shelf of the Aegean Sea presents itself as a single unit. Article 6 of the Geneva Convention stipulates that the delimitation of the shelf between two states shall be the middle line between the two coasts. The borderline in the Aegean Sea thus runs halfway between the Turkish coast and the Greek islands

Until 1973, these provisions had been theoretical, legal considerations without material consequences for Greek-Turkish relations. The oil discoveries at Thasos changed this thoroughly. In view of the global energy crisis, Ankara reacted immediately: on 1 November 1973, the Turkish government granted the state oil company exploration and exploitation licences for the Aegean continental shelf. At the same time, the Turkish government gazette published a map showing the boundary line of the alleged Turkish shelf in the northern Aegean. This line ran west of the Greek islands from Samothrace via Limnos, Agios Efstratios, Chios to Psara and Antipsara. Ankara thus laid claim to the shelf area east of this line, outside the 6 nm zone of the Greek islands for itself, a shelf area that Greece considered its own and for which it had already granted some exploration licences.

Athens formally rejected these claims on 7 February 1974, referring in particular to Articles 1 and 6 of the Geneva Convention on the Law of the Sea. Ankara responded on 27 February by stating that the Geneva Convention did not apply in this case because Ankara had not signed it.[2] The Greek islands did not have a continental shelf of their own, but merely sat on the East Aegean continental shelf, which was a continuation of Anatolia. The border between the Greek and the Turkish shelf is the middle line between the two coasts. mainland coasts. At the same time, Ankara called on Greece to negotiate.[3]

At the end of March 1974, the situation worsened during a NATO manoeuvre. Turkish military aircraft entered Aegean airspace without reporting to Greek military air control, al-

---

1 In this context, an interview in the daily newspaper Hurriyet with retired General Bedrettin Demirel from 3 July 1986 is of interest. German text in: *Zypern Bulletin,* Nr. 1 5, (7. August 1986), p.3.

2 Article 1 of the Geneva Convention stipulated that the term continental shelf refers to:"'(a) to the seabed and subsoil of the submarine areas adjacent to the coast but outside the area of the territorial sea, to depth of 200 meters or beyond that limit, to where the depth of the superjacent waters admits of the exploitation of the natural resources of the saicl areas; (b) to the seabed and subsoil of similar submarine areas and subsoil of similar submarine areas adjacent to the coasts of islands". Islands are defined according to the second UN Convention on the Law of the Sea as follows: Article 121: (1) An island is a naturally formed area of land, surrounded by water, which is above water at high tide. (2) Except as provided for in paragraph 3, the territorial sea, the contiguous zone, the exclusive economic zone and the continental shelf of an island are determined in accordance with the provisions of this Conventien applicable to other land territory. (3) Rocks which cannot sustain human habitation or economic life of their own shall have no exclusive economic zone or continental shelf". Quoted from: *The Status Qua in the Aegean,* p. 13.

3 Article 6 of the Geneva Convention stipulated: "Where a continental shelf adjoins the territorial sea of two or more States whose coasts are opposite each other, these States shall demarcate by mutual agreement the parts of the shelf belonging to them. In the absence of agreement, the boundary line shall be the median line through all points equidistant from the nearest points of the baselines from which the breadth of the territorial sea of each of these States is measured, unless special~circumstances justify the fixing of a different boundary line". Quoted from: Association of Editors of Athens Daily Newspapers ,ed., *Bedrohung in der Agäis.* (Athen, n.d.), p. 21.

though according to NATO regulations in force at the time, the Aegean was under Greek air control. Greek interceptors pushed the Turkish aircraft away and the NATO manoeuvre was aborted.

At the beginning of April, Ankara announced that exploration work would soon begin in the Aegean Sea outside Greek territorial waters. On 8 May, Athens stressed its peaceful intentions but would resist attacks on Greece's territorial integrity. On 9 May, Turkish Foreign Minister Günes declared that Ankara wanted to maintain peaceful relations with Athens, but that the Aegean should not become a Greek sea. Finally, on 25 May, Athens agreed to negotiate on the shelf issue, on the basis of the Geneva Convention. On 29 May, Günes announced the dispatch of a research vessel to the "Turkish" part of the shelf waters. Although the research vessel would be accompanied by navy vessels, this was not to be understood as an attack on territorial integrity. The research vessel, the Candarli, escorted by 32 navy vessels, set course for the disputed area on 29 May and took magnetometric measurements there until 4 June. Greece put its naval forces on alert.

On the same day, Ankara informed Athens that it was ready to negotiate without preconditions, i.e. without reference to the Geneva Convention. Nevertheless, on 6 June, Ankara granted the TPAO new drilling licences for the area north of Limnos. Athens responded on 14 June by protesting against the Candarli trip and certain aggressive statements by Turkish politicians. At the NATO meetings in Ottawa on 20 June and in Brussels on 25/26 June, the foreign ministers of Greece and Turkey discussed the relations between the two countries. Ankara proposed the establishment of two committees to negotiate jurisdiction over the Aegean shelf and the status of minorities in both countries and Cyprus. Athens, however, rejected this, fearing prejudice.

On 27 June, Ecevit announced that his government would continue with its exploration programme, but that it had no aggressive intentions towards Greece. On 8 July he again called on Athens to negotiate and on 10 July he announced that he had rejected the Greek response of 14 June and would continue with the explorations. On 17 July, the Turkish government Gazette published another map showing the so-called middle division line between Greece and Turkey. Ankara thus laid claim to the entire shelf area east of this line, leaving out only the territorial waters, i.e. 6 nm, of the Greek islands. According to Ankara's interpretation, the islands did not possess a shelf of their own. Further developments were drawn into the maelstrom of events on Cyprus.

Obviously encouraged by the successfully completed invasion of Cyprus, Ankara now turned more strongly to its second expansion objective in the Aegean by expanding the previous conflict and enriching it with further aspects. Depending on the opportunity, this or that aspect was played into the foreground, but the actual aim, the expansion in the Agaeis, was kept in mind. The conflict in the Aegean became so complex that even experts lost sight of the bigger picture. No wonder that parts of the Western European public fell for the Turkish propaganda theories, which were repeated often enough and sounded plausible, and did not take the Greek statement that they felt threatened by Turkey seriously or dismissed it as Athenian propaganda. In addition, the Greek counter-arguments were of a dry legal nature and were not "sold" cleverly enough until the early 1980s. The following remarks will attempt to present these individual aspects according to their chronological occurrence, to make the respective problems transparent and to outline their development through brief longitudinal sections.

After the landing on Cyprus, the Turkish Civil Aviation Authority notified the regional office of the International Civil Aviation Organisation (ICAO) on 20, 23 and 29 July that parts of the eastern Aegean airspace were to be declared dangerous zones and thus closed to civil air traffic. When Athens protested against this, Ankara withdrew the NOTAM (Notice to Airmen), only to issue a new warning on 6 August under the designation NOTAM 714. NOTAM 714 required all aircraft to report to Turkish air control in Istanbul after flying over a line approximately in the middle of the Aegean Sea to communicate their position and flight plan. Only in this way would it be possible for the Turkish military radar to distinguish between peaceful civilian aircraft and possible attackers. Athens refused to accept this NOTAM. It contradicts the ICAO statutes because Ankara is trying to unilaterally extend its area of control. Moreover, the line requested by Ankara strangely corresponds to the "centreline" requested in relation to the shelf. For its part, Athens declared the Aegean a dangerous area on 14 August with NOTAM 1066 and 1152, for which it would no longer assume responsibility for the coordination and management of air traffic. On the same day (14 August), Athens declared its withdrawal from the military part of NATO. Before outlining further developments, it seems useful to make some basic remarks on the problem of air control at this point.

The constantly growing air traffic had prompted the convening of an international conference on civil aviation in Chicago as early as the end of 1944. The 37 participating states signed a treaty that regulated international air traffic in broad outline. After 26 states ratified this treaty, the ICAO (International Civil Aviation Organisation) was founded in 1947 and the world was divided into regional organisations. The organisation responsible for the Aegean is the European Mediterranean Regional Air Navigation Organisation. This organisation defined the boundaries of its sub-organisations, the Flight Information Regions (FIR) in the European-Mediterranean area, at two conferences in Paris in 1952 and Geneva in 1958, in which both Greece and Turkey participated.[1]

The following arrangement was found for the airspace of the Aegean: Athens FIR was to control the entire airspace up to the beginning of Turkish national airspace. Athens thus controlled both the national airspace over the Greek islands and the international airspace of the Aegean. In this context, control meant that every civil and military aircraft flying west from Turkey was obliged to report to the Athens air traffic control centre one or two minutes after crossing the Turkish coast and to give its flight plan and position. From then on, the Athens air traffic control took over the direction of the rest of the flight. Aircraft flying eastwards reported to the flight control in Istanbul after leaving the Athens FIR in order to receive instructions from there. Control within an FIR extends only to purely technical air traffic control and must not be confused with air sovereignty over one's own national territory. An FIR usually extends far beyond the area of national air sovereignty.

The Turkish requirement (NOTAM 714) of 4 August now demanded that every eastbound aircraft report to air traffic control in Istanbul after crossing the centre line of the Aegean, i.e. both Greek internal flights from Athens to the eastern Aegean islands and Greek Air Force flights in the same airspace.

However, Ankara's demand did not only concern the ICAO regulations, but also the NATO air security and control system. The NATO air control areas were congruent with the FIRs, i.e. the military protection of the FIR area of Athens was under the control of Greece. Early warning, air defence and tactical operations in this area were the responsibility of NA-

1 Article 1 of the Chicago Convention read:
The contracting States recognize that every State has the comso grenzen plete and exclusive sovereignty over the air space above its einvernehmlich territory
.. Article 2 determined:
For the purpose of this Convention the Punkten der territory of a State shall be deemed to be the land areas and "as each territorial waters adjacent there to under the sovereignty, suzeraine protection or mandate of such State. Quoted after: *The Status Quo in the Aegean,* p.14.

TO's 28th Tactical Air Fleet, the Greek Air Force. Ankara's NOTAM 714 thus also challenged NATO command structures. But back to the chronological development.

Athens informed ICAO on 13 September 1974 through NOTAM 1157 that it declined all responsibility for flights in the Aegean. International airlines then suspended all direct flights between Greece and Turkey and no longer used the airways crossing the Aegean. However, these measures primarily harmed Turkey's air traffic with Europe, as it now had to be routed around the closed FIR, essentially through the Bulgarian FIR.

Attempts by ICAO to mediate in October 1974 initially failed due to Turkish intransigence. On Greek initiative, direct air traffic between Greece and Turkey was resumed in the spring of 1975, but NOTAM 714 remained in force. It was not until February 1980 that Ankara lifted NOTAM 714, as the economic effects of the closure of the Aegean airways became too tangible. Instead, Ankara had found another institution with the help of which it could assert its claims to air control over the Aegean: NATO.

Until the Greek NATO partial withdrawal, there had been two united NATO headquarters in Izmir (Smyrna) under American generals, LANDSOUTHEAST and the 6th ATAF (Allied Tactical Air Force). The Turkish and Greek air forces were under the command of the 6th Tactical Air Force. After the Greek partial withdrawal from NATO, the Turkish military air traffic control area was apparently extended westwards into the Aegean Sea with NATO's blessing. Ankara interpreted this expansion of its control area very generously.

In 1931, Greece had set the limits of its national airspace off the mainland coasts and the islands at 10 nm.[1] Until 1975, Ankara had not objected to this, as it was in line with international regulations. According to these, every country has the right to extend its airspace to a maximum of 12 nm,[2] i.e. to the limit of its territorial waters. Greece's 10 nm are thus secured under international law according to the principle of the "greater right". Now Ankara demanded that Greek airspace be withdrawn to 6 nm corresponding to Greek territorial waters in the Aegean. To lend weight to its demand, Turkish military aircraft constantly flew over the disputed airspace in the East Aegean from then on. Athens always protested when its national airspace was violated and therefore cancelled several NATO exercises in recent years.

The fact of the unilateral change in military air control areas became visible when Athens signalled its readiness to return to NATO at the end of 1977. It quickly became clear that a simple re-establishment of the two united NATO commands was out of the question in view of the continuing conflict between Greece and Turkey. NATO High Command therefore decided to establish two separate commands, one in Izmir and one in Larissa. The only controversy remained the demarcation of the operational zones of the two air commands (6th ATAF

---

1 By Decree of the President of the Hellenic Republic:
Decree". Zitiert nach: *The Status Quo in the Aegean,* p. 14.
"The Greek Republic, having regard to Articles 2 and 9 of Act No.5017 regulating civil aviation, published in the Government Gazette, part No. 153 of 13 June 1931, and to Article 1 of Act No. 2569 of
19 April 1921 ratifying the International Aviation Convention (of Paris signed on 13 October 1919), published in the Government Gazette, No. 68 of 26 April 1921, and upon recommendation of the Minister of Aviation, has resolved and decreed as follows: The extent of the territorial waters referred to in Article 2 of Act No. 5017 shall be fixed at ten sea miles from the coast of the State. The Minister of Aviation shall be responsible for publishing and giving effect to this Decree". Quoted from: The Status Quo in the Aegean, p. 14.

2 Article 1 of the Chicago Convention read:
The contracting States recognize that every State has the complete and exclusive sovereignty over the air space above its rnehmlich territory. Artikel 2 bestimmte: For the purpose of this Convention the territory of aState shall be deemed to be the land areas and territorial waters adjacent thereto under the sovereignty, suzerainty, protection or mandate of such State.
Quoted from: *The Status Quo in the Aegean,* p. 14.

in Izmir, 7th ATAF in Larissa). Ankara demanded the maintenance of the status quo and Athens the return to the status quo ante.

Athens feared that agreeing to the expansion of Turkish military air control space would prejudice the FIR and the shelf problem. In 1980, when NATO Supreme Commander Haig put forward a plan to return to the status quo ante, Ankara vetoed it. Athens did the same when Haig made a proposal that accommodated Turkish wishes. In 1980, the new NATO Supreme Commander Rogers made a new proposal for a solution, which Athens again rejected because it favoured Turkey.

Only when Foreign Minister Mitsotakis threatened in 1980 that Greece would leave NATO altogether and close the US bases did the Americans put pressure on Ankara. The result was the so-called Rogers Agreement, which stipulated a return to the status quo ante in peacetime. The Athens FIR and the NATO airspace were again congruent in peacetime. To all appearances, however, Rogers must have made the concession to Ankara that after Greece's return to NATO, bilateral negotiations would still take place on the delimitation of air defence areas in the event of conflict. This would mean that even in NATO manoeuvres certain parts of the East Aegean, i.e. also Greek islands, would come under the operational control of the Turkish side. Since Athens regarded this as a possible precedent for the other points at issue, it flatly rejected these conditions and refused to set up the Larissa headquarters until this question had been finally settled in the sense of establishing the status quo ante.[1] Since Ankara refused to do so, NATO will probably have to manage without the new headquarters for some time yet.

Ankara, on the other hand, continued its policy of systematic violation of Greek airspace in the East Aegean until very recently. Obviously, the aim is to keep the question of military air control open and to make Athens a "troublemaker" in the alliance by protesting to the NATO High Command. The continuation of the invasion of Cyprus in the second half of August 1974 made Athens fear further Turkish landings on the East Aegean islands, and they therefore hurriedly began to fortify the islands closest to the Turkish coast and moved troops there in larger numbers. The Athenian fears were reinforced by statements from Turkish politicians of all colours. For example, on 17 January 1975, Turkish Prime Minister Sirmak stated that half of the Aegean belonged to Turkey. On 20 January 1975, Defence Minister Sancar announced Turkish claims to the Greek islands in the East Aegean. On 22 January, Foreign Minister Esenbel added that Cyprus had been the first step towards the Aegean. In April, the new Foreign Minister Caglayangil reaffirmed that half of the Aegean belonged to Turkey. And another source said that Rhodes could become a second Cyprus. Statements of this kind have been made by almost all prominent Turkish politicians until very recently. Unsurprisingly, the Greek government pushed the defence of the East Aegean islands by all means. No sooner had the first news about this reached the public than Ankara was already protesting against it through diplomatic steps, government statements and a press campaign: Greece was violating international treaties by fortifying the islands and was preparing a military aggression against the Turkish mainland. The treaties mentioned in this context are the Treaty of Lausanne and the Paris Peace Treaty between the Allies and Italy, which ceded the Dodecanese to Greece. The Treaty of Lausanne divided the East Aegean islands into two groups. Above the Greek islands of Samothrace and Limnos and the Turkish islands of Imbros (Gökcada) and Tenedos (Bozaada), which lie at the exit of the Dardanelles, Article 4, paragraph 3, stipulated that they

1 Spotlight, Nr. 29, (15.0ctober 1985), p. 3.

should be demilitarised. At the Montreux Conference (June/July 1936), Turkey regained full sovereignty over the straits; at the same time, the demilitarised status of the four aforementioned islands was lifted. It should be noted in this context that Greece was also one of the signatory states of Montreux. After the signing of the Montreux Treaty, the Turkish ambassador in Athens, Essref, assured the Greek government in an official letter on 6 May 1936 that Ankara agreed to the remilitarisation of Samothrace and Limnos,[1] and the Turkish Foreign Minister at the time, Rüstü Aras, stated during the ratification debate of the Turkish Parliament that the Treaty of Lausanne with its demilitarisation provisions had been repealed seilS6- Ankara itself began fortifying its islands immediately after the signing of the convention. Greece followed suit in December 1936.

With regard to the islands of Lesvos, Chios, Samos and Ikaria, Article 13 of the Treaty of Lausanne stipulated that no naval bases or fortifications could be built there, but that the stationing of armed forces equal to the number of local conscripts and an adequate gendarmerie unit was permitted.[2] In other words, the Treaty of Lausanne also allowed for certain defence measures. How had this come about?

During the debates in Lausanne itself, the following difference of opinion emerged: Ankara demanded total demilitarisation for these islands. It was countered that in such a case these islands would be at the mercy or disgrace of Turkey. To avoid this, corresponding demilitarised zones would have to be created on the Anatolian side. Since this was impracticable, partial armament was agreed to. According to Article 14 of the Paris Treaty between the Allies and Italy, the Dodecanese was to retain a demilitarised status, but this did not exclude the presence of police forces.[3] Turkey was not a signatory state to this treaty and therefore has no right under international law to make any demands regarding the remilitarisation of the Dodecanese islands. Athens has so far apparently avoided transferring regular army units to the islands, but has increased the gendarmerie forces to such an extent that there is hardly any difference between them and armed forces.

However, Greece can point to a higher legal right to justify its defence efforts, namely the right of every country to self-defence as laid down in Article 51 of the UN Charter.

---

1 The decisive passage read: "Turkey would look favourably upon every measure that the Greek Government would consider necessary to take to ensure the security of the islands that are under the sovereignty of Greece ... The militarisation of the Greek islands that will take place is that of the islands of Samothrace and Lemnos.

We absolutely agree to the militarisation of the two islands and at the same time to that of the Straits. Quoted from *The Status Quo in the Aegean*, p. 7.

2 Parliamentary Debates Vol. 12, p. 309; 5. Legislature, 81st Session, Friday 31. July The text of the declaration read "The provisions concerning the islands Lemnos and Samothrace belonging to our neighbour and friend Greece, which had been demilitarised in application of the Lausanne Treaty of 1923 are also abolished by the Treaty of Montreux and we are very glad of that. I avail myself of this opportunity to stress once more that one of the characteristics of the policy of new Turkey is to wish for her friends what she wished for herself and not to wish for her friends what we would regard as an injustice for ourselves". Quoted from: *The Status Quo in the Aegean,* p. 7.

3 Artikel 1 3 des Vertrages von Lausanne lautete:
"With a view to ensuring the maintenance of peace, the Greek Government undertakes to observe the following restrictions in the Islands of Mytiline, Chios, Samos and Nikaria:
No naval base and no fortification will be established in the said islands.
Greek military aircraft will be forbidden to fly over the territory of the Anatolian coast. Reciprocally. the Turkish Government will forbid their military aircraft to fly over the said islands.
The Greek military forces in the said islands will be limited to the normal contingent called up for military service, which can be trained on the spot, as weil as to a force of gendarmerie and police in proportion to the force of gendarmerie and police existing in the whole of the Greek territory". Quoted from: *The Status Quo in the Aegean,* p. 5.

If there had ever been any doubt as to whether the aggressive declarations of Turkish politicians were merely verbal radicalisms, the establishment of a 4th Turkish Army with headquarters in Izmir, announced on 20 July 1975, provided clarity. This so-called Aegean Army has been systematically expanded in recent years and is not under NATO high command. According to American information, it currently comprises about 35,000 men, i.e. 2 infantry divisions, 1 regiment of "leathernecks", commando and paratrooper units of unknown strength. In addition, there are a large number of transport helicopters[1] and approx. 50-60 naval landing craft from a total of 80 in Turkey.

The manoeuvres carried out by the 4th Army in recent years were landing operations. Since such operations are only conditionally envisaged in the NATO defence concept for the region, it was natural that Athens interpreted these manoeuvres as preparations for landing operations on the Greek islands lying off the Turkish coast and was now for its part pushing the military expansion of these islands. Furthermore, the recent equipping of the 4th Army with a large number of inflatable assault boats, which could be used for landing purposes over short distances, e.g. against Samos or individual Dodecanese islands, had a worrying effect.

Athens, however, did not leave it at securing the islands militarily, but tried to gain the backing and support of its allies through diplomatic actions.

When negotiations between the US and Greece began in April 1976 on the extension of the US base agreement in Greece, Foreign Minister Bitsios demanded as a precondition for the extension an American guarantee of the Greek borders against a possible attack by Turkey and US support in solving the Cyprus problem. US Secretary of State Kissinger was not prepared to accept this junctim, but he wrote a letter assuring Greece of active support in the event of Turkish provocations or use of force; moreover, the US would contribute to a just solution of the Cyprus problem. Although this letter was not binding under international law and was soon forgotten, it showed the new direction of Greek foreign policy: the USA and NATO were to be held responsible.

This tactic became clear during the negotiations on Greece's return to NATO: in 1977, Karamanlis demanded that NATO commit itself to helping solve the Cyprus problem. After Greece's return to NATO in 1980, Athens demanded a fixed ratio of US military aid to Turkey and Greece of 7:10 and a border guarantee against Turkey, otherwise the base agreement would not be renewed.

Finally, in 1981, after his election victory, Andreas Papandreou demanded a NATO guarantee, as the US government had rejected one, and the establishment of the 7:10 ratio. When Papandreou realised in the course of further negotiations that a border guarantee could not be obtained, he insisted on the establishment of the 7:10 ratio, which was also established in September when the new base agreement was concluded: The USA undertook to maintain the existing balance of power in the Aegean. In addition, Papandreou succeeded in mobilising the Graeco-American minority in the USA during the negotiations and forming their representatives into a pressure group in Congress that could not be ignored. Attempts by the Reagan administration in 1984 and 1985 to shake the 7:10 ratio promptly failed in Congress.

Athens also operated quite cleverly at the NATO level. In 1979, Ankara had demanded that the islands of Limnos, Agios Efstratios and Samothrace be removed from NATO defence planning. NATO's Supreme Allied Commander Europe rejected this demand, but at the request of NATO Secretary General Luns, who was reasonably said to have pro-Turkish sym-

1 Article 2 specified: "These islands shall be and shall remain demilitarised." Quoted from: *The Status Quo in the Aegean,* p. 10.

pathies,[1] it was politically decided that Limnos should henceforth be excluded from NATO exercises because its military status was not clear. This decision led Athens to declare that it would boycott NATO manoeuvres in the Aegean until the Alliance recognised Greek sovereign rights over Limnos.

When Athens announced national manoeuvres in the North Aegean in September 1984, which included Limnos, Ankara protested strongly and denied Greece's right to do so. Athens responded by transferring the Greek army and air force units stationed on Limnos (one infantry brigade and two fighter squadrons) to NATO in November 1984. Ankara vetoed this at the NATO defence ministers' meeting in Brussels on 3 December 1984. Athens countered by preventing the subordination of Turkish units to NATO through its veto. This created the grotesque situation that in 1985 neither Greek nor Turkish troops were formally subject to NATO. The same process was repeated in November 1985, despite the mediation attempts of the new NATO Secretary General, Lord Carrington. [2]

Finally, in January 1985, Papandreou announced a new defence doctrine that directed the focus of Greek defence efforts to the east, since Greece was more threatened from there than from the north. Over the next few months, Greece prepared for parliamentary elections, which took place on 2 June 1985 and from which Papandreou again emerged victorious.

After the election victory, Papandreou initiated a new phase of Greek policy. On the one hand, the particular vulnerability of the Aegean islands was taken into account by establishing a ministry for these islands, and on the other hand, Athens began a diplomatic offensive.

In January 1986, the Minister of the newly created Ministry for the Aegean Islands held his first press conference, in which he spoke, among other things, about the defence of the islands, in which the civilian population was integrated.[3] During the next few months, Athens tried to make its position on the Aegean issue clear in talks with representatives of the US State Department (John Whitehead and Rozanne Ridgway), the British Foreign Secretary Sir Geoffrey Howe, US Secretary of State George Shultz and Lord Carrington.

On 22 May, Defence Minister Giannis Charalambopoulos explained the Aegean problem, in particular the Umnos issue, to the NATO Defence Planning Group gathered in Brussels and reiterated the Greek proposal to place the Greek units stationed on Limnos under NATO control. The NATO planning group responded positively by accepting Athens' proposal to station an independent US brigade on Umnos in case of conflict. Ankara irritably accused NATO of raising tensions between Ankara and Athens. At the same time, a campaign against NATO Supreme Commander Rogers began in the Turkish press and Turkish politicians again issued threats.[4]

Athens fought back by raising the whole problem at the EC summit in The Hague at the end of June 1986. Even before the EC summit, Papandreou informed the European heads of government in such an objective way about the individual aspects of the Greek-Turkish conflict in a detailed letter of 14 June that the EC Commission President Jacques Delors confirmed that the problems had been understood. At the summit itself, Papandreou again urgently warned against the danger of a Greek-Turkish war.[5]

---

1 Turkish newspapers noted in this context that Luns had been a friend of Turkey; Carrington could not be expected to be similarly positive set. *Spotlight,* Nr. 31, (15 November 1985), p. 1.

2 *Spotlight,* Nr. 31, (15 November 1985), p. 1.

3 *Greece. Background. News. Information.* Nr.6. (London. 30. Januar 1986), p. 2.

4 *Athen News Agency,* (23. Mai 1986); *Greece.Background, News, Information,* Nr. 10, (19. Juni 1986).

5 *Greece. Background, News, Information.* Nr. 11, (17. Juli 1986); *Athens News Agency,* (27., 28., 29. Juni 1986).

Papandreou also let it be known that Athens had reservations about Ankara's desire to revive its association agreement, which had been frozen after the Turkish military took power in September 11. Before the Association Agreement can be reinstated, Ankara must respect human rights in Cyprus and give up its occupation. In particular, Ankara must repeal a law from 1964 that is still in force and prohibits the sale, inheritance and transfer of Greek property in Turkey. In July and August, Athens made further attempts to block the opening of negotiations on the revival of the Association Agreement[1] or the granting of EC aid to Turkey.[2] In mid-September 1986, the Greek Deputy Foreign Minister Theodoros Pangalos repeated the Greek concerns to the EC Association Council . Parallel to the manoeuvres in the EC, Athens continued its efforts to gain international support for its position.

Ankara responded to these Greek diplomatic actions by holding manoeuvres in the Aegean, with the associated provocations going beyond the usual, such as a Turkish destroyer firing live ammunition at the Cypriot passenger ship City of Limassol. In view of the negative publicity in the international press, Ankara shifted the focus of its anti-Greek policy back to primarily civilian targets, i.e. Cyprus. After this digression, let us return to the more military aspects of the conflict, the shelf problem.

On 27 January 1975, Athens took the initiative by proposing to Ankara to submit the shelf issue to the International Court of Justice in The Hague. Ankara agreed on 6 February and proposed to start bilateral high-level negotiations to prepare the case.Nevertheless, the Turkish prime minister let himself be heard on the radio the next day, saying that the explorations were continuing.

Although this project did not come to fruition at first because the Norwegian company from which Ankara had chartered a research vessel refused to take seismic measurements in the disputed areas, Ankara continued to make efforts, as statements by members of the government proved. On 6 April 1975, Demirel stated that the delimitation of the shelf would have to be determined through bilateral negotiations. On 16 April, Foreign Minister Caglayangil announced the motto according to which Ankara acted from then on: "Let's negotiate, maybe we can reach an agreement, but let's not go to The Hague! A political solution, then, instead of a legal one.

Nevertheless, Caglayangil and Bitsios met in Rome on 19 May for initial talks about going to The Hague together. On 31 May 1975, Karamanlis and Demirel met at the NATO summit in Brussels. They agreed that the work of the lawyers should be accelerated in order to be able to submit the case to the International Court of Justice as soon as possible. Both sides signed a communiqué on this, in which they also stressed that the disputed issue should be resolved peacefully.[3]

---

1 *Athens News Agency,* (17. September 1986).

2 The text of the communiqué read: In the course of their meeting the two Prime Ministers had an opportunity to give consideration to the problems which led to the existing situation as regards relations between their countries. The decided that these problems should be resolved peacefully by means of negotiatiations and as regards the continental shelf of the Aegean Sea by the International Court at The Hague. They defined the general lines on the basis of which the forthcoming meetings of the representatives of the two Governments would take place. In that connection they decided to bring forward the date of the meeting of experts concerning the question of the continental shelf of the Aegean Sea and that of the experts on the question of air space. The two Prime Ministers agreed that efforts should be made on both sides to create and maintain a good atmosphere in relations between Greece and Turkey so that existing problems might be resolved and co-operation between the two countries re-established to their mutual advantage.
Finally, the two Prime Ministers agreed they would give their support to the intercommunity negotiations in Vienna. 135

3 Griechenland Informationen, Nr. 6, (Bonn, Februar 1975).

Over the next few months, the legal experts met on the one hand and Ankara established the 4th Army on the other. In September 1975, Demirel announced that the work of the experts would be stopped for the time being. Obviously, Ankara wanted to avoid going to The Hague together.

Over the next few months, the Aegean issue became Turkey's domestic bone of contention. Opposition leader Ecevit accused Demirel of squandering Turkish opportunities. Athens would only negotiate seriously under pressure. Demirel then announced in February 1976 that a hydrographic research vessel (Sizmik 1) would soon be sent to the area of the island of Thasos, where the Greeks had found oil three years earlier. Athens responded by proposing that Turkey conclude a non-aggression pact. Demirel initially welcomed this, but when the opposition attacked him massively, he rejected the proposal.

In the following weeks, Athens warned Ankara several times that a dangerous situation would arise if the Sizmik 1 entered Greek shelf areas. Ankara replied that if Athens obstructed the passage of the Sizmik 1, measures would be taken. The Sizmik finally entered the area west of Lesbos on 6 August 1976, escorted by a single Turkish minesweeper, and left again on 9 August. Both sides were obviously anxious to avoid a clash and kept a low profile. Nevertheless, Athens turned to the Security Council on 10 August and requested a special session. At the Security Council meeting, both sides presented their known positions. The Security Council adopted Resolution 395/1976, which appealed to both adversaries to reduce tensions, start negotiations and 'bring the whole case before the International Court of Justice. Athens welcomed the resolution. Ankara agreed to start bilateral negotiations but refused to go to The Hague.

Athens then submitted two requests to The Hague: 1. that the Court issue an interim injunction prohibiting both countries from carrying out further research in the disputed waters in the Aegean Sea and from taking military measures that could threaten the peace of the region. 2. that the Court clarify the principle of the shelf issue.

The Court rejected the first request, saying that the Turkish actions did not constitute a serious prejudice.

Athens then agreed to resume bilateral negotiations pending a ruling on the second application. On 14 October 1976, The Hague asked both sides to submit the case. Athens welcomed this, Ankara refused, questioning the competence of the court. Finally, in January 1979, the court made its decision: it declared itself not competent in the matter. This closed the judicial route to a solution and a bilateral solution had to be found.

The corresponding negotiations had already yielded a first result in September 1976 between Caglayangil and Bitsios in New York: Confidential expert talks would be started in Bern with the aim of delimiting the shelf of both countries. On 2 November 1976, the negotiations began in Bern. On 11 November, the delegations signed the so-called Bern Declaration. The negotiations were to be conducted strictly confidentially and seriously, and in any case a result was to be sought. During the negotiations, neither side would take any action that could prejudice the outcome of the negotiations. Both sides would refrain from any polemics against the other. The negotiations would be based on international law. A committee of experts should negotiate.

It makes little sense to trace the negotiations that followed, as they have not produced any concrete results to date. Ankara kept repeating its well-known theses on the shelf, and Athens kept referring to its positions secured under international law, which were further underpinned in 1982 by the decisions of the 2nd Conference on the Law of the Sea. Ankara did not join this agreement either and derived rights to the Aegean shelf from this fact. Although nothing decisive has happened on the shelf issue in recent years, Ankara has endeavoured to keep the question open, as the dispatch of a research vessel to the Aegean in July 1986 shows.

The Cyprus Problem after 1974

Ankara took a similarly intransigent stance on the Cyprus problem. In November 1974, at the request of the non-aligned countries, the UN General Assembly unanimously passed a resolution calling on all states to respect the sovereignty, independence and territorial integrity of Cyprus. All foreign troops should be withdrawn. The constitution of Cyprus must apply to both communities. Direct negotiations between the two communities should be resumed and the UN Secretary General should facilitate them. Although these talks were resumed, Ankara ignored the UN's more far-reaching demands.[1]

In early February 1975, the Cypriot government under Kliridis presented a plan that corresponded almost exactly to the Turkish demands of August 1974. An independent sovereign republic was to be created on the basis of a bicommunal, multiregional federal state under a strong central government with a few purely Turkish cantons in the north, whose total area was to amount to about 18 percent. In addition . there should also be some other small Turkish enclaves in the south. The right of free movement of both ethnic groups had to be guaranteed. However, the Turkish side rejected this proposal and three days later, on 13 February 1975, proclaimed the north of Cyprus an independent federal state.[2] When the Cypriot government protested against this at the UN, Turkey indicated that it would ignore any resolution that was contrary to its interests.[3]

However, the intercommunal talks under the auspices of the UN Secretary General continued. The Turkish Cypriot side (Denktash) responded to the Kliridis proposal with a proposal for the creation of a confederation with a weak central government.[4] Although Makarios repeatedly signalled his unwillingness to compromise, it took until January 1977 for direct talks to be held between Makarios and Denktash in the presence of the UN Secretary--General's Special Representative, de Cuellar. Makarios accepted the federal solution, provided that freedom of movement and the right to settle and own property were not restricted. Denktash, on the other hand, offered to reduce the size of the Turkish-occupied zone. At a second meeting on 12 February 1977, in the presence of UN Secretary General Waldheim, Makarios and Denktash reached an agreement on the guidelines for further inter-communal negotiations

Cyprus should become an independent, non-aligned, bi-communal federal republic. The division of the territory of the two ethnic groups should take into account the economic potential, the productivity and the former land ownership. The central government would be given

1 *Griechenland Informationen*, Nr. 6, (Bonn, February1975).

2 According to Denktash's latest statements, he already wanted to proclaim an independent state at that time, but Ankara forbade him from taking this step.. *Günaydin Kibris,* 15. November 1988.

3 *Ibidem*, No. 9, (April 1975}.

4 *Das Zypernproblem. Historische Obersicht und Analyse der jüngsten Entwicklungen.* (Nikosia, 1982), p. 20. The original text read: 1. We are seeking an independent, non-aligned, bi-communal Federal Republic. 2. The Territory under the administration of each community should be discussed in the light of economic viability or productivity and landownership. 3. Questions of principles, like freedom of movement, freedom of settlement, the right of property and other specific matters, are open for discussion, taking inot consideration the fundamental basis of a bi-communal federal system and certain practical difficulties which may arise for the Turkish Cypriot community. 4. The powers and functions of the ventral Federal Government will be such as to safeguard the unity of the country, having regard to the bi-communal character of the State.

the competences necessary to maintain the unity of Cyprus, taking into account the bi-communal character of the state.[1]

Makarios was thus prepared to accept the ethnic and administrative division of the island, provided that the federal character was preserved. But it was precisely here that views diverged. While the Greek Cypriots wanted the territorial question to be solved largely analogous to the numerical strength of the ethnic groups and demanded a federal state with a strong central government, the Turkish Cypriots strove for the territorial status quo to be largely maintained, for a confederation with a weak but equally staffed central power.[2]

Although the inter-communal talks in Vienna were resumed in March 1977, they did not produce any concrete results, since the Turkish Cypriot side refused to make concessions on the territorial issue in particular. Even when, after Makarios' death (August 1977), the Turkish side made concrete proposals for the first time at the inter-communal talks in April 1978, it became apparent that it was stubbornly sticking to its line: A loose confederation of two states with equal rights should be formed. The new state should have two parliaments, two constitutions, two governments and two armies. At the federal level, both sides should be equally represented in all organs. The foreign policy of the federal government should not interfere with the right of the federal states to conclude treaties with foreign states, especially with the respective mother country. Finally, the Turkish side offered about 5 per cent of the island territory for restitution.[3]

The new President of Cyprus Kyprianou stated in this regard that these proposals were only meant to legalise the fait accompli created by the Turkish occupation.[4] Nevertheless, the ethnic group talks were resumed, which after several interruptions led to direct negotiations between Kyprianou and Denktash in May 1979. In the presence of UN Secretary General Waldheim, agreement was reached on further concrete negotiations on the basis of the Makarios-Denktash Agreement of February 1977, which, however, were soon interrupted again

1 Ronald Meinardus, "Eine neue Phase im Zypern-Konflikt", *Europa Archiv,* Folge 10, 19849, p. 299.

2 *Archiv der Gegenwart,* {20. April 1982}, p. 25.526.

3 *Griechenlandinformationen,* r. 37, (Juni 1978).

4 *Archiv der Gegenwart,* (20. April 1982), p. 25.528. Specifically, the scheme provided for the following:136 1. It was agreed to resume the intercommunal talks on 1 5 June 1979.

1. It was agreed to resume the intercommunal talks on 1 5 June 1979.
2 The basis for the talks will be the Makarios-Denktasch guideline of 12 February 1977 and the United Nations resolutions relevant to the Cyprus question.
3. There should be respect for human rights and fundamental freedoms of all citizens of the Republic.
4. The talks will deal with all territorial and constitutionalzu diesem aspects. ter Ankara
5. Priority will be given to reaching agreement on the resetter 1988. lement of Varosha under United Nations auspices simultaneously with the beginning of the consideration by the interlocutors of the constitutional and territorial aspects of a comprehensive settlement. After agreement on Varosha has been reached, it will be Implemented without awaiting the outcome of the discussion on other aspects of the Cyprus problem.
6. It was agreed to abstain from any action which might jeopardize the outcome of the talks, and special impor tance will be given to initial practical measures by both s;des to promote good will, mutual confidence and the return to normal conditions.

The demilitarization of the Republic of Cyprus is envisaged, and bi-communal matters relating thereto will be discussed.

The independence, sovereignty, territorial integrity and non·.community alignment of the Republic should be adequately guaranteed against productiunion in whole or in part with any other country and against any form of partition or secession. Ffreedom of 9. The intercommunal talks will be carried out in a continuing and latters, are sustained manner, avoiding any delay.10. The intercommunal talks will take place in Nicosia.

when it became clear that the Turkish side understood bizonality to mean the division of the island.

In April 1980 Waldheim said that the failure of the intercommunal talks was essentially due to three causes: 1. the Turks demanded their own state, which should only be loosely connected with the Greek-Cypriot one in a confederation. 2. in the Turkish view, the question of the security of their national community had to be linked with the territorial problem. 3. the Turkish side was only prepared to negotiate if the Greek Cypriots renounced some of their demands.[1]

Although the inter-ethnic talks were resumed again and again, they remained in vain. On 24 May 1981, parliamentary elections were held in the free part of Cyprus. Parliamentary and presidential elections followed in June in the Turkish north of Cyprus. Obviously, the two--state status of the island was to be documented in this way. In August 1981, the Turkish side once again submitted a proposal that contained no new elements and was promptly rejected by Kyprianou: One would accept a federation, but not a confederation or two separate states, as this would mean the division of the island. The inter-communal talks were useful, but the real problem, which concerned the whole world, was Ankara's occupation policy. However, this was not even discussed at the inter-communal talks.

The first concrete result of Athens' new foreign policy was UN Resolution 37/253 of 13 May 1983, which called on Ankara to immediately withdraw its occupation forces from Cyprus.[2]Ankara shot back by saying that this resolution was neither legally nor politically valid. Denktash described it as "aggression against the island Turkish community", cancelled his further participation in the community talks and threatened to proclaim an independent state in Northern Cyprus.

In August 1983, the new UN Secretary General, Peres de Cuellar, made a new attempt to get the conflicting parties to talk by submitting a memorandum with a negotiating framework. After some hesitation, the Greek Cypriot side agreed.[3] However, Denktash rejected de Cuellar's proposals and demanded a "summit meeting" with President Kyprianou. At the same time, he issued a kind of ultimatum: if the Greek Cypriot side was not prepared to negotiate on the "basis of equality", they would proclaim their own state.

Despite Kyprianou's willingness to meet with Denktash, the latter carried out his threat of secession on 15 November 1983 with the proclamation of the "Turkish Republic of Northern Cyprus". Although the readiness for further negotiations on the creation of a "real" federation was immediately signalled, at the same time the "president of the new state announced that the two-state status of the island was not to be shaken. The 1977 agreement between Makarios and Denktash on the unity of the country had become obsolete. It seems that he took advantage of the government crisis in Ankara to take this step. Ankara then had no choice but to recognise Denktash's state.[4]

Immediately after the proclamation of the new state, Prime Minister Papandreou and President Kyprianou met to coordinate their policies. They agreed on the following three objectives: Condemnation of the secession by the international community, non-recognition of the "phantom state" and withdrawal of the declaration of independence.[5]

---

1 *Ibidem*, p. 25.528.

2 Meinardus, *op..cit.,* p. 301.

3 The resolution was adopted with 103 votes in favour, 5 against and 20 abstentions.

4 The position of the Cypriot government on de Cuellar's proposals can be found in: *Zypern Bulletin,* Nr.5, (5. März 1984).

5 Meinardus, *op.cit..,* p. *302.*

The first two aims of Athens and Nicosia were achieved: the Security Council, in Resolution 541/83, condemned the secession as legally invalid, demanded its revocation and called on all states not to recognise the new state. The summit conference of the Commonwealth countries, the European Community, the European Council, the European Parliament and others condemned Denktash's action. Even the superpowers were united in their condemnation of the secession. No state in the world except Turkey recognised the "Turkish Republic of Northern Cyprus". However, the third aim, the withdrawal of the secession, was not achieved.

In January 1984, Kyprianou submitted to Secretary General de Cuellar a framework plan for a possible solution to the Cyprus problem. The fundamental point was the complete demilitarisation of Cyprus. After the ~bz~g of all Turkish occupation troops, all troops stationed there under the Treaty of Guarantee (Greek and Turkish) would also have to be withdrawn and the Cypriot National Guard and the so-called Turkish-Cypriot armed forces disbanded. An international force under UN auspices should take over the security of the island externally and internally. The independence, territorial integrity, sovereignty and non-alignment of Cyprus must be guaranteed by an international treaty; neither Greece nor Turkey should become a guarantor.

Cyprus should become a federal state. All arrangements were to be based on the UN resolutions and the "summit agreements" between Makarios-Denktash of 1977 and/or the Kyprianou-Denktash agreements of 1979. 25 per cent of the island's territory was to come under Turkish-Cypriot administration. In the central executive, the Turkish ethnic group was to be represented with 30 per cent, but it had to be ensured that any government activity could not again be blocked by an absolute veto. On the question of the legislatures, the framework plan offered two alternatives, assuming that mechanisms for conflict resolution were provided for. This was followed by a catalogue of federal powers, which indicated that the federal component should be strongly developed. Finally, freedom of movement, establishment and property were called for.[1]

Although this framework plan contained substantial concessions, Denktash rejected the territorial concessions as too small and demanded that Turkey remain Cyprus' guarantor power.[2] Nevertheless, de Cuellar and Kyprianou continued their attempts to restart the inter--ethnic talks. On 16 March 1984, de Cuellar and Denktash met, with the former asking the Turkish Cypriot leader to comment on Kyprianou's framework plan. Denktash promised to do so but delayed his response, announcing instead on 10 April that a referendum on the constitution of Northern Cyprus would be held in August.[3] Alarmed by this development, de Cuellar sent his special envoy, Hugo Gobbi, to Cyprus for consultations on 15 April. Denktash denied de Cuellar's right to make any proposals and indicated that he was seeking a meeting with Kyprianou as leader of the Greek Cypriot state and himself as president of Northern Cyprus. At the same time, he announced that Ankara would accredit an ambassador to Northern Cyprus on 17 April and was expecting an ambassador from Northern Cyprus.[4] There was no mention of a response to Kyprianou's framework plan.

Thus provoked, the Cypriot government requested the convening of the Security Council. At its meeting on 11 May, Resolution 550/84 was passed, condemning Denktash's actions and

1 Günaydin Kibris, 15. November 1988.
2 *Ibidem,* p.305.
3 The text of the Framework Agreement can be found in: *Zypern Bulletin,* Nr. 10, (15. Mai 1984), p. 4f.
4 *Spotlight,* Nr. 1, (18 May 1984), p. 1

calling on the Secretary General to intensify his efforts to resolve the Cyprus problem.[1] De Cuellar therefore re-established contact with both sides and after protracted preliminary negotiations, during which Denktash trickily tried to enhance the value of his "government",[2] the negotiating delegations met separately with de Cuellar in Vienna on 6 and 7 August. The Secretary General handed both sides a working paper with certain proposals that could later form a basis for negotiations and asked them to submit their answers to him by 10 September.[3]

Both sides responded positively and talks began in New York on 10 September. De Cuellar negotiated separately with both delegations. Further such indirect negotiations took place in October and November 1984. In January 1985, they met again without result, as Denktash deliberately torpedoed the talks by ultimatley demanding that de Cuellar's working paper, which had been revised in the meantime, not be discussed but signed.[4]

At the beginning of April, de Cuellar made a new attempt. He forwarded a document to both sides which entered the discussion under the name "single consolidated draft agreement". In it, the Secretary General had summarised the main positions of earlier documents. He invited both sides to comment on it. Kyprianou accepted it as a basis for discussion. Denktash did not reply at first, but snubbed the General Secretary by holding a referendum on the *constitution" of his state (on 5.5.85) and presidential elections (on 9.6.85). In July and August Denktash explained his position even further: both ethnic groups had to be completely equal. Bizonality must be complete (Denktash mentioned the two German states in this context). The guarantee by Turkey was indispensable, and in order to guarantee this, Turkish troops would have to remain stationed in Cyprus in considerable strength.[5]

Despite Denktash's intransigent attitude, de Cuellar made every effort to get the talks going again. After various meetings with representatives of the Cypriot government and with Denktash in the summer and autumn of 1985, it was decided to continue the talks at a lower level with the Turkish Cypriot side in London and the Cypriot government in Geneva. The aim of the negotiations was to work out a text of a framework plan acceptable to both sides. In parallel to these negotiations, Nicosia and Athens continued to seek international support quite successfully. On 2 September 1985, the Non-Aligned Conference gathered in Luanda called on Ankara to withdraw its occupying forces and Denktash to withdraw its secession, and on 13 September the European Parliament condemned Denktash's ~ actions.[6] This was followed in October by the condemnation of the Commonwealth Conference.[7]

Parliamentary elections were held in Cyprus on 8 December, and on 10 December Kyprianou repeated his proposal to completely demilitarise Cyprus. The Turkish troops would have to be withdrawn and replaced by an international peacekeeping force - Kyprianou thus rejected a dictum by Denktash that the precondition for further negotiations was that the Greek Cypriot side tolerate the presence of Turkish troops on the island.

In January 1986, the Soviet Union submitted a plan for solving the Cyprus problem within the framework of an international conference, which was broadly in line with the ideas of Ni-

---

1 *Zypern Bulletin,* Nr.8, (16. April 1984), p.1.
2 *Zypern Bulletin,* Nr. 9, (30. April 1984), p. 2.
3 The text of the resolution can be found in: *Zypern Bulletin,* Nr.10, (15. Mai 1984).
4 He demanded that his representative at the talks be recognised by de Cuellar as Foreign Minister and that Austria recognise the Northern Cypriot passports.*Spotlight,* Nr. 6, (1.August 1984), p. 7.
5 *Zypern Bulletin,* No. 15, (22 July 1985) and *Greece. Background, News. Information.* Nr.3, (17. October 1985).
6 *Zypern Bulletin,* Nr. 18, (18 September 1985).
7 Zypern Bulletin, No. 16, (7 August 1984).

cosia and Athens, which is why it was warmly welcomed there.[1] Ankara did not want to hear of the Soviet proposal and Denktash agitated that the interference of the superpowers in the internal affairs of Cyprus was not in the island's interest.

In the meantime, further negotiations had taken place between the two sides, which apparently brought about a certain convergence of positions again. On 31 March, de Cuellar therefore submitted a third solution plan (draft framework agreement). In its basic substance, it did not differ significantly from its predecessors, but it did differ in the envisaged chronology of its implementation. De Cuellar wanted to solve the territorial and constitutional problems in the first phase. Only after these problems had been solved, but partly at the same time, were the Turkish troops to be withdrawn.

After intensive consultations between Athens and Nicosia, the Cypriot government rejected the settlement plan, fearing renewed intervention if Turkish forces remained (Turkish Prime Minister Özal 'stated that Turkey's rights as a guarantor power could not be negotiated) and that the settlement of the three fundamental freedoms contained in the plan was considered unsatisfactory.[2] Kyprianou called instead for the convening of an international Cyprus conference or a "summit" with Denktash to negotiate the outstanding issues.[3]

Özal, on the other hand, said that if the Cyprus question was not resolved soon, his country would reassess the situation. Denktash, undeterred, did not want to participate in any international conference until Northern Cyprus was recognised as a state.[4] Ankara had obviously opted for a tougher approach. Özal's "state visit" to Northern Cyprus at the beginning of July and the temporary closure of the borders of Northern Cyprus can be seen as elements of this new policy.

Nicosia also brought these provocations to the attention of the public, most recently at the Non-Aligned Conference in Harare, but a change in the attitude of Ankara and Denktash was not achieved. Indirect contacts through the UN Secretary General have been resumed, but a solution is certainly not in sight this way, as the past has shown.

Meanwhile, other facts have been created in the north that deepen the division of Cyprus. Shortly after the occupation of Cyprus, Ankara began to shift the demographic composition of the island's population in favour of the Turkish element. By the end of 1986, some 40,000 new settlers from Anatolia had been brought to Cyprus, increasing the Turkish share of the population by about 38 per cent. The intention behind this is clear: the Turkish share of the Cypriot population was to be increased to such an extent that in future negotiations this higher figure would have to be taken as a basis and possibly a retention of the occupied territories by the North could be justified. When this colonisation policy was denounced internationally, the new settlers were declared to be returnees of Turkish-Cypriot origin. Later new settlers came as agricultural helpers, but they were soon provided with the necessary papers. In contrast to the Turkish Cypriot expellees from the south of Cyprus, the new settlers were given housing and land from former Greek possessions. This naturally led to tensions between island Turks and new settlers, especially since the army supported the new settlers.

Initially, the Turkish Cypriot population had welcomed the presence of the Turkish troops quite unreservedly. In view of the preferential treatment of the new settlers, the initially cordial relationship cooled down. In addition, resentment arose from the confrontation of the

---

1 Text of the Soviet proposal in: *Zypern Bulletin,* Nr.3, (27 January 1986).

2 Greece.Background, News, Information, No.9, (19 June 1986), p.2.

3 *Zypern Bulletin,* No. 9, (28. April 1986), p.1; the text of Kyprianou's reply can be found in: *Zypern Bulletin,* Nr. 13, (23 June 1986), p.2f.

4 Zypern Bulletin, No.10, (12 May 1986), p.1 and No. 11, (26 May 1986), p.4.

different cultural and civilisational levels of the two groups. Recently, extensive consumer tourism from the mainland to Northern Cyprus , where the standard of living is higher, has angered the business community, as payment is made in Turkish lira instead of foreign currency.

All this did not affect the relationship with the motherland very much, as the memory of the difficult time before 1974 prevailed for the time being, but even among apologists and official representatives of the North there are now voices that would welcome the Turkish army leaving, provided of course that the security needs of the island Turks are met. Obviously, the idea that the army could stay forever and that Northern Cyprus could one day be annexed is also a source of concern for this group of people.

The minorities problem

The third complex of the Greek-Turkish conflict, the conflict over Thrace, has hardly been taken note of in Europe.

As is well known, in 1923 the Treaty of Lausanne had agreed on the most extensive exchange of populations between Greece and Turkey. Only the Greek minority of Istanbul and the inhabitants of the islands of Imbros and Tenedos, as well as the Islamic minority of Western Thrace, were excluded from the exchange. The text of the treaty granted both minorities full minority protection and the islanders extensive local self-government. According to the Treaty of Lausanne, there was to be a balance between the two minorities. In 1934, Istanbul's Greek minority comprised about 110,000 people. Approximately 10,000 Greeks lived on the islands of Tenedos and Imbros.... The Muslim minority of Thrace, consisting of Turks, Pomaks and Gypsies (Roma), numbered about 106,000 people. The current numbers are: Approx. 5,000 Greeks in Istanbul and approx. 1,000 on both islands combined. The figures for the Muslim minority in Western Thrace vary between 100,000 and 130,000. The balance of the two minorities enshrined in the Treaty of Lausanne has thus changed to the disadvantage of the Greek minority. As mentioned, the exodus of Greeks began during the Second World War and increased in the 1950s and 1960s in parallel with the escalation of the Cyprus conflict, accompanied by pogroms of such a degree that one may speak of "expulsion~ and a "breach" of the Treaty of Lausanne.[1]

The Muslim minority in Greece, on the other hand, was treated liberally until the military junta (in contrast to the Slavic minority) and not harassed out of reciprocity. It was only under Papadopoulos that repressive measures began in the form of state intervention in the social and economic affairs of the Turkish minority according to the principle of "tit-for-tat". Although the character of Athens' minority policy changed again towards liberalisation after the return to democracy, the principle of reciprocity has not yet been completely abandoned.

Ankara has recently played up the ethnic tensions in Thrace as "systematic oppression of the Turkish minority", but overall one gets the impression that the whole Western Thrace complex serves Ankara only as a diversionary tactic.

The Soviet attitude

The main aim of Soviet, as previously of Tsarist foreign policy, is to achieve direct access to the Mediterranean. The maximum objective is to become a littoral state either by itself or through an allied state. The minimum aim is unhindered access for merchant and warships

1 Isabelle Guisan, "Die letzten Byzantiner gehen in aller Stille unter", *Pogrom,* Nr. 123, (1986), p. 46ff.

from the Black Sea to the Eastern Mediterranean through the Dardanelles in times of peace and war.

Given the geostrategic realities of the region, the maximum aim could only be achieved by integrating the Balkan states or Turkey into the Soviet sphere of influence; the minimum aim would require a change in Turkey's attitude. The opponent of this Russian aspiration to the Mediterranean was traditionally Great Britain until 1947 and then the USA within the framework of the Truman Doctrine.

With regard to the maximum target, the situation in the interwar period was as follows, greatly abbreviated: Great Britain had strategic control over the eastern Mediterranean as part of the Empire's lifeline. Between the Soviet Union and the Mediterranean lay a ring of independent Balkan states that were either allied with France or supported by Britain. An attempt by the Soviet Union to achieve the maximum objective would have meant a conflict with the Western powers and was thus out of the question.

But there were also two obstacles in the way of achieving the minimum goal: Turkey's traditionally anti-Russian stance and, again, above all, British policy.

The Ottoman Empire's centuries-long defensive struggle against the Russians had created a trauma on the Turkish side that, like the Turkish trauma in Greece, continues to have an effect to the present day. The short-term rapprochement between the two states following the First World War did little to change this.

In 1919, after the collapse of the Ottoman Empire, the Western Allies had occupied Constantinople and the Straits and supported the Russian counter-revolutionaries from there. In the peace treaty 'of Sevres (1920), among other things, the Straits were placed under the control of the Allied Straits Commission, and Smyrna and its hinterland -..had to be ceded to Greece. In view of the impending confrontation with the Allies and the Greeks, the new Turkish leader Kemal concluded a friendship pact with the Soviet Union in March 1921 under the slogan of common opposition to Western imperialism. The purpose of the pact was mutual backing against the Allied interventions.

In the Lausanne Peace Treaty, Ankara regained sovereignty over the Straits, but the Western powers prohibited their fortification and closed them to the passage of warships even in peace. Britain had successfully defended its hegemony in the Mediterranean.

This was followed in 1925 by the Soviet-Turkish Treaty of Friendship and Neutrality, which again has to be seen in the light of the respective backlash against foreign intervention; it was valid until 1945. When at the Montreux Straits Conference the Soviet Union raised the desire for free passage of its warships, it was successfully blocked by British-Turkish interplay.

During the Second World War, Ankara managed to remain neutral until February 1945 by carefully manoeuvring between Germany and the Allies - but by the summer of 1944, things were back in flux. The Red Army was preparing to overrun the entire Balkan region. Prime Minister Churchlll was highly alarmed, for a Balkans under Soviet control threatened the British lifeline across the Mediterranean. In that infamous Percentage Agreement of October 1944 with Stalin, Churchill successfully prevented the Soviet maximum solution: Greece and Yugoslavia would not be part of the Soviet sphere of influence.

Although the neutral status of the Straits had been a source of annoyance for the Allies during the war and had led to considerations of changing it in favour of the Soviet Union after the end of the war, in 1945 corresponding Soviet demands met with the massive rejection of Ankara and from 1946 also of the Americans, who in the meantime had begun to build up their maritime presence in the eastern Mediterranean. In 1947, the Truman Doctrine followed, in the framework of which Turkey was developed into an ani-communist bulwark. In 1950,

Turkey participated in the Korean War, as did Greece, and in 1952 both countries joined NATO. Soviet-Turkish relations had reached a low point. Thus, even the Soviet minimum objective was obviously not realisable in the long term.

After Stalin's death, Moscow initiated a new policy. The Soviets officially retracted Stalin's demands for the eastern Turkish territories of Kars and Ardahan[1] and made cautious overtures to Ankara, but during the UN debates on Cyprus in the late 1950s, Moscow supported the Greek position through its allies. The motives were transparent: Moscow wanted to prevent a NATO solution to the Cyprus problem and at the same time disrupt the cohesion of the Western alliance. Neither manoeuvre, however, led to any significant change in Moscow's relations with Ankara and Athens.

After the establishment of the Republic of Cyprus, Moscow adapted its course to the new circumstances and supported Nicosia's independence course. A non-aligned Cyprus was in the Soviet interest, and as long as Cyprus was independent, Moscow could indirectly exert its influence through AKEL. Moreover, if Cyprus were to be annexed to Greece, AKEL would have been banned in a similar way to the Greek Communist Party (KKE). Accordingly, Moscow concluded a trade agreement with Nicosia in December 1961. [2]

The first direct interference of the Soviet Union in the Cyprus problem occurred in connection with the second Cyprus crisis at the end of 1963. As we have already mentioned, Moscow intervened at Nicosia's request and prevented the integration of Cyprus into NATO planned by the USA in February 1964 by threatening to intervene. In connection with the renewed escalation of the Cyprus crisis in August 1964, Khrushchev repeatedly repeated his warnings against intervention. The Soviet Union would help Cyprus defend its freedom and independence. A conflict near the Soviet southern border would not leave the Soviet Union indifferent.[3]

The letter from Johnson to Inönü of June 1964, quoted earlier, in which he forbade the Turkish prime minister in a rather rude tone to interfere in the Cyprus question, opened up new, unexpected possibilities for Soviet policy. Inönü was very annoyed by the tone of the letter and felt abandoned by the USA and NATO in the Cyprus question[4]. Out of disappointment, he initiated a new Turkish policy towards the Soviet Union.

Moscow reacted by, on the one hand, continuing to support Nicosia in its course of non-alignment and, on the other hand, trying to exert influence on Ankara. In September 1964, a Cypriot delegation visited Moscow, where an economic agreement and a treaty on military aid were signed, in the framework of which the Cypriot Gendarmerie was later supplied with weapons from the CSSR.[5]

In October 1964, a Turkish foreign minister visited the Soviet Union for the first time in twenty years. Foreign Minister Erkin and his Soviet colleague Gromyko formulated in their communiqué regarding the Cyprus problem that they were both in favour of a peaceful solution, respect for territorial integrity and independence for the recognition of the existence of two ethnic groups . This statement showed that Moscow was still cautious in its tactics and for the time being only against Enosis.

---

1 Udo Steinbach, "Neuere Entwicklungen in den politischen Beziehungen zwischen der Sowjetunion und der Türkei, Griechenland und Zypern"', *Osteuropa,* (1973), p. 532.

2 Vangelis Koufoudakis, I Kypros kai oi yperdynameis 1960 -1979, in: *Kypros. Istoria, provlimata kai agones tou laou tis.* Edited by G.Tenekidis and. G. Kranidiotis, Athen 1981, p. 372.

3 *Keesing's Contempoary Archives*, p. 20,266

4 *Ibidem,* p. 20,500

5 *Keesing's Contemporary Archives*, p. 20.266.

In January 1965, a delegation of the Supreme Soviet led by Presidium member Nikolay Podgornyj visited Turkey. On a nasty occasion, Podgornyj became much more explicit. He explicitly recognised the rights of the two Cypriot ethnic groups, which was received with satisfaction in Ankara. At the end of January, Foreign Minister Gromyko added to the Soviet position. In an interview with Izvestia on 20 January, in which he spoke about the Cyprus question, he did not rule out a federal solution.[1]

In May 1965, Gromyko made a return visit to Ankara. Ankara's high expectations regarding the Cyprus question were disappointed; Gromyko did not go beyond the formula found by Podgornyj in January. Moscow kept a similar low profile during the state visit of Prime Minister ürgüplü; it remained with Podgornyj's formula.[2]

In the next two years, Soviet-Turkish economic relations strengthened, but there were no changes in the Cyprus question. This also applied to Kossygin's state visit in December 1966 and Demirel's return visit in September 1967.

At the same time, in the UN debates on Cyprus, Moscow demanded that the UN decisions be respected and supported the island's independence. Obviously in order not to lose its credibility in the eyes of Ankara, Moscow gave the CSSR the task of supplying the Cypriot gendarmerie with weapons. All in all, until 1967 Moscow pursued a policy on the Cyprus question that was, strictly speaking, contradictory in itself.

During the years of the Greek military dictatorship, there was a shift in emphasis. As the signs of a bilateral agreement between Ankara and Athens grew to the disadvantage of Cyprus, Moscow repeatedly warned against attacks on Cyprus's independence. Finally, in 1971, Makarios visited the Soviet Union, which assured him of its firm and active opposition to any interference by imperialist forces,[3] which then provided substance to the propaganda against Makarios as "Castro in a priest's skirt". Since the Soviet position also implicitly questioned Turkey's right to intervene as a guarantor power, the Soviet Union made a "good-will gesture" in 1972. It sent Podgorny, who had meanwhile been elected head of state, on a state visit to Ankara in April. The published final communique emphasised the good neighbourly relations. On Cyprus, it noted that both countries were in favour of a peaceful solution to the Cyprus problem and rejected enosis. Cyprus's independence, sovereignty and territorial integrity must be respected, as well as the legitimate rights and interests of the communities. Both states demanded the continuation of the inter-ethnic talks, which should be conducted on the basis of equality.[4]

In February 1972, when the Greek military junta ultimatley demanded from Makarios the delivery of the arms supplied by the CSSR to the UNFICYP and shortly after Grivas launched the EOKA-B actions, Moscow opened a large-scale propaganda campaign against the imperialist interference in Cyprus.[5]

In the meantime, the Soviet wooing of Ankara had begun to pay off. Ankara interpreted the provisions of the Montreux Straits Convention extensively and allowed the passage of Soviet warships in such numbers that the Soviet Union could build up its "Eskadra" in the Mediterranean. During the Arab-Israeli October War of 1973 (Yom Kippur War), the Soviet Union was able to supply its friends with supplies relatively easily because Ankara allowed

---

1 Nuri Eren, "Die türkisch-sowjetischen Beziehungen". *Europa Archiv,* 9, (1965), p. 337; Friedrich-Wilhelm Fernau, "Nachbarschaft am Schwarzen Meer", *Europa Archiv,* 17, (1967), p. 616.

2 Keesing's ContemporaryArchives, p. 20.371.

3 *Ibidem,* p. 20.500.

4 Koufoudakis, *op.cit,* p. 374.

5 Steinbach, *a.a.O.,* p. 536.

Soviet aircraft to fly over Turkish territory on their way to Syria. In contrast, American planes were not allowed to fly to NATO airfields, except those in Portugal.[1]

During the Cyprus crisis in July and August 1974, the internal contradictions of Soviet Cyprus policy became apparent. Despite its previously frequently publicised willingness to stand up for Cyprus's independence, Moscow remained remarkably reticent throughout. It was quite obvious that the Soviets, as Kissinger had correctly foreseen, shied away from direct confrontation with the USA. But also vis-à-vis Athens and Ankara, the Soviet Union pursued a restrained course and limited itself to activities within the framework of the Security Council and to propaganda. Thus, it joined in the condemnation of the Sampson coup, but abstained in the condemnation of the first Turkish invasion.

The situation of Soviet foreign policy became even more difficult when the military junta in Greece fell, a democratic government was formed and Athens withdrew from the military part of NATO. While this development was very welcome to Moscow, it also increased the dilemma of Soviet foreign policy. If the Soviet Union sided with Athens on the Cyprus and Aegean issues, it was upsetting Ankara and failing to take advantage of the opportunities offered by the American arms embargo on Turkey. If it supported Ankara, it might drive Athens back into the arms of NATO. Faced with this dilemma, Moscow opted for a course of internationalising the Cyprus question and called for the convening of a conference of Security Council powers with those involved in the conflict, which the US refused to do. Even as the Turkish invasion continued in August, the Soviet press did not attack Ankara directly, but condemned the "NATO" intervention in Cyprus.[2]

In the following years, Moscow stuck to this course. On the one hand, it propagated the independence of Cyprus and repeatedly demanded the convening of an international conference. On the other hand, it maintained its bilateral relations with Turkey and tried to establish similar ones with Greece. In December 1975, Soviet Premier Kossygin visited Ankara to deepen the rapport with Turkey. However, Ankara found the Soviet proposals too far-reaching and rejected the proposed text of a joint declaration. Nevertheless, the Soviet Union continued its efforts to develop good neighbourly relations with Turkey. Ankara rewarded the Soviet courtship over the next few years by interpreting the Montreux Convention broadly and even allowed heavy units of the Soviet fleet to pass through the Dardanelles. After the second American arms embargo, Ankara retaliated by prohibiting the American air force from entering a 120-mile-wide restricted area along the Soviet-Turkish borders in 1982. Soviet planes bringing supplies to Iraq after the outbreak of the Iran-Iraq war, on the other hand, were allowed to fly over Turkish territory.

Despite this bilateral rapprochement, the Soviet Union was tactful in the Cyprus question and avoided taking sides unilaterally. This became clear in June 1978 during Prime Minister Ecevit's visit to Moscow. In the joint final communique, nothing new was found with regard to the Cyprus question.[3]

In October 1979, Karamanlis became the first Greek prime minister ever to visit the Soviet Union. Although the Soviets treated him with great courtesy, he was unable to persuade the Soviet leadership to change course on the Cyprus question. The visits of Papandreou and Özal to Moscow in 1984 and 1986 were similarly fruitless. The Soviet Union was not prepared to be drawn into the Greek-Turkish conflict on one side or the other. In January 1986, it docu-

1 Kadritzke, *a.a.O.,* p. 78.
2 Kadritzke, *a.a.O.,* p. 78.
3 Koufoudakis. *a.a.O.,* p. 292.

mented this once again when it submitted a concrete proposal for a solution, which was welcomed by Nicosia and Athens but rejected by Ankara.

The Greek-Turkish Conflict since 1986

Developments up to February 1987

Since the completion of the first part of this paper in autumn 1986, developments have taken place which give rise to hopes that a solution to the Greek-Turkish conflict may yet be found. The occasion for this new positive development was a near clash between Greece and Turkey in March 1987.

The first significant foreign policy event after the summer break was the signing of a quasi friendship treaty with Bulgaria by Papandreou on 11 September. Although it was emphasised that the "treaty" was not directed against third parties, it was very clear that it was also seen by both countries as a kind of flank protection against possible Turkish aggression. The text stated that if a situation arose that was perceived as threatening by both countries, contact would be established immediately and joint consultations would be held on ways to avert the danger.[1] A promise that, as was to be shown in connection with the March crisis of 1987, did have substance

In mid-September, further efforts were made by Greek and Cypriot diplomacy within the UN framework, which differed little from the previous ones, except that they had the full approval of the Soviet Union. On 16 September, Athens gave the EC Association Council to understand that before the Association Agreement with Turkey could be revived, Ankara would first have to settle its conflict with Greece and withdraw its troops from Cyprus. Finally, in October, the usual NATO exercises took place in the Aegean, in which Greece again did not participate and in which the almost obligatory airspace violations and the subsequent Greek protests took place.

At the same time, the Greek and Cypriot governments sought to clarify their position at every possible opportunity. It would be idle to list these activities, as they all basically pursued the same objective: the preservation of the diplomatic status quo.

On 20 November, however, a direct diplomatic confrontation between Greece and Turkey took place that seems worth recording. On that day, the Turkish Foreign Minister Halefoglou took over the chairmanship of the Foreign Ministers' Commission of the Council of Europe. The theme of the meeting was the situation of human rights and refugees in the world. State Secretary Kapsis took the opportunity to point out the different views on human rights violations within the member states of the Council of Europe. A harmonisation of legislation was urgently needed.

Although Kapsis had not mentioned Turkey by name, Halefoglou reacted. He accused Greece of constantly attacking Turkey. Kapsis, on the other hand, said that he had not mentioned Turkey, but that Halefoglou's response confirmed that his country was an example of human rights violations. The Turkish Foreign Minister had demanded direct dialogue between Athens and Ankara to settle the bilateral conflict. Greece was ready to open dialogue at any time, on one condition: Ankara must make a binding declaration that it recognises the status quo in the Aegean. The dialogue had already been initiated at ambassadorial level, but had been interrupted by the proclamation of the Turkish-Cypriot pseudo-state. If Turkey intends to redraw the Greek borders, there is only one answer: Greece does not lay any claim to Turkish soil, but will not cede one centimetre of Greek land, sea or air space. Let's start the dialogue immediately, in the adjoining room. Let's start with the critical issue of the withdrawal of

1 *Athens News Agency,* 12 September 1986.

Turkish forces from Cyprus," Kapsis ended. Halefoglou had nothing to say on the matter- Papandreou argued similarly at the EC summit in London and Defence Minister Charalambopoulos at the meeting of NATO Defence Ministers in Brussels in early December: dialogue with Turkey was only possible if Ankara withdrew its troops from Cyprus and recognised the status quo in the Aegean - Papandreou repeated this view on the occasion of the visit of Spanish Prime Minister Felipe Gonzalez on 9 December. On 19 December, an incident provoked by the Turkish side occurred at the border river Evros, in which one Greek and two Turkish soldiers were killed. Although both sides tried not to play up the incident, Özal used the opportunity to offer Athens the opening of dialogue again. Athens responded by referring to its known conditions. On 31 December, State Secretary Kapsis specified that the shelf problem was not a political but a legal one. Athens was immediately prepared, together with Ankara, to submit the case to the international court. The Turkish government spokesperson did not elaborate on this in his reply. Instead, he accused Greece of steering an anti-Turkey course. Over the next few days, the two government spokespersons exchanged more verbal jibes, but then the Evros incident was forgotten in the face of new issues. For the next few weeks, Greek foreign policy was preoccupied with US military aid to Turkey and Greece. The US administration tried to deviate from the legally prescribed quota of 7:10 in favour of Turkey for the 1988 budget year. Athens mobilised the American-Greek Pressure Group in Congress, which promptly became quite active over the next few weeks.

On 3 January 1987, Papandreou addressed the Economic Forum in Davos. Among other things, he expressed his hope that Ankara would eventually withdraw its occupation forces from Cyprus and give up its claims on Greece in the Aegean. Then nothing would stand in the way of mutually beneficial Greek-Turkish economic cooperation.[1] Although Papandreou warned only a few days later that if Ankara advanced further in Cyprus it would mean war, one gets the impression that this statement was not meant too seriously. Papandreou had apparently taken a conciliatory course. The following episode also speaks for this.[2]

At the beginning of February, the international oil consortium NAPC (North Aegean Petroleum Company), which is 70 percent controlled by the Canadian Denison Mines Company, but which also includes a subsidiary of BASF (Wintershall), had let it be known that it planned to drill test wells east of Thasos in the near future, as the previous exploitation field "Prinos" was expected to dry up in the early 1990s. The Greek government, apparently not wanting any unnecessary confrontations with Turkey, then announced a law that would allow NAPC to be brought under the control of the state oil company DEP by buying up 25 per cent of its shares, which would ultimately allow the Greek state to determine the company's course. On 24 February, NAPC went public: NAPC would start drilling test wells 10 sea miles east of Thasos on 28 March. The company does not need permission from the Greek government. It has the right to do so under its oil and gas contract. The Greek government could only prevent it from drilling by declaring a state of emergency in the area concerned. Otherwise, the price offered for the shares is an insult.[3]

Industry Minister Peponis responded on 26 February. He rejected the accusation that Greece was nationalising foreign companies. The case was political and not economic. There were special circumstances; Peponis referred to Turkish politics. Greece had the right to decide where to drill. If the Denison Company refused to give up part of its shares voluntarily,

1 *Athens News Agency,* 21 November 1986 and *Spotlight,* No. 47, Dezember 1986.

2 *Athens News Agency*, 2 February 1987

3 *Athens News Agency,* 25 February 1987

a law would be passed allowing for a forced sale for adequate compensation in foreign currency.[1] This was tantamount to a ban on drilling.

The NAPC then mobilised the diplomatic missions of the companies involved. On 27 February, the ambassadors of the USA, Canada and the FRG, accompanied by the Secretary of State of the Canadian Ministry of Foreign Affairs, Stanford, intervened at Peponis and expressed their hope that a mutually satisfactory solution could be found. Until then, the conflict was between the Greek government and the international consortium, which had broken out because Athens wanted to avoid a conflict with Turkey provoked by the drilling projects.

Ankara, however, did not honour the Greek position. On the same day (27 February), the Turkish ambassador in Athens, Nazmi Akiman, lodged an official protest: Greece would hopefully respect the Berne Declaration. The Greek Foreign Ministry replied that the Berne Declaration was inoperative. Moreover, it was Greece's business to decide where, when and how drilling on the Greek shelf would be undertaken. In Ankara, acting Prime Minister Erdem (özal was in the US for medical treatment) stated that drilling within 10 nautical miles of Thasos violated the Berne Declaration. *"The Turkish government is monitoring with due attention activities, involving the continental shelf which extends beyond the two countries' territorial waters, and will not overlook such activities"*. On 1 March, it was announced that the Turkish oceanographic research vessel Pirj Reis had left Izmir for research in the Aegean Sea.

Athens rejected Ankara's accusations with the familiar arguments, called on Turkey to submit the case to the International Court of Justice and stated that the Berne Declaration had become inoperative with Turkey's breaking off of negotiations in September 1981.

For a better understanding of the problems associated with the so-called Berne Declaration, we reproduce the full text here:

MINUTES ON THE PROCEDURE TO BE FOLLOWED FOR THE DELIMITATION OF THE CONTINENTAL SHELF BETWEEN GREECE AND TURKEY

1. The two parties agree that the negotiation shall be frank, thorough and conducted in good faith, with a view to reaching an agreement based on their mutual consent concerning the delimitation of the continental shelf between them.

2 Both parties agree that this negotiation shall, by its nature, be strictly confidential.

3 Both Parties reserve their respective positions with regard to the delimitation of the continental shelf.

4 Both parties undertake not to use the provisions of this document and the proposals to be made by either party in the course of these negotiations under any circumstances outside the context of these negotiations.

5 Both parties agree that there shall be no statements or leaks to the press on the content of the negotiations, unless they agree otherwise by mutual consent.

6. Both parties undertake to refrain from any initiative or action relating to the EEZ continental shelf which might prejudice the negotiations.

7 The two Parties undertake, with regard to their bilateral relations, to refrain from any initiative or act which would tend to discredit the other.

8 The two parties have agreed to study the practice of States and the international rules in this field, with a view to identifying certain principles and practical criteria which could be used in the case of the delimitation of the continental shelf between the two countries.

---

1 *Athens News Agency*, 27 February 1987.

9 To this end, a joint commission shall be set up, which shall be composed of national representatives.

10 Both parties agree to adopt a gradual pace in the process of negotiation to follow, after consultation between them.[1]

In the following days, the Piri Reis, accompanied by a naval vessel, left Turkish territorial waters, but remained in international waters and returned to the Turkish sovereign zone. During this process, she was constantly observed by the Greek air force. Athens, however, saw no reason for alarm yet. On 5 March, Ankara escalated the verbal conflict. The ,spokesman of the Turkish Foreign Ministry, Yalim Eralp, claimed that the entire Aegean Sea outside the respective territorial waters was "disputed territory". If Greece violates the Berne Declaration, Turkey will take all necessary steps to protect its interests and rights in the Aegean, he said. Greek government spokesperson Kourtis called on Eralp to show more restraint and invited Ankara to take the case to the International Court of Justice, as all peace-loving nations would do in such a case. [2]

On 6 March, the Greek government introduced a bill in the Greek parliament on the forced participation of the Greek state oil company DEP in NAPC. The bill called on NAPC to start negotiations with DEP immediately. If this did not happen within two months, the Greek state would proceed to compulsory acquisition through the DEP. From the moment the law enters into force, all activities in the deliberate sea areas would be prohibited.[3]

On 9 March, Ankara escalated the tensions. The spokesperson of the Foreign Ministry, Eralp, repeated the well-known Turkish positions and accused Greece of expansionist plans. The Greek government spokesman, Roubatis, sha rply rejected this: it was grotesque that the

---

1

PROCES-VERBAL SUR LA PROCEDURE A SUIVRE POUR LA DELIMITATION DU PLATEAU CONTINENTAL ENTRE LA GRECE ET LA TURQUIE

1. Les deux parties sont d'accord pour que la negociation soit franche, approfondie et conduite de bonne foi, en vue d'aboutir ä un accord base sur leur consentement mutuel en ce qui concerne la delimitation du plateau continental entre elles.
2 Les deux parties sont d'accord pour que cette negociation soit,de par sa nature, strictement confidentielle.
3 Les deux parties reservent leurs positions respectives en ce qui concerne la delimitation du plateau continental.
4 Les deux parties s' engagent ä ne pas utiliser les dispositions de ce document et les propositions qui seront faites de part et d'autre au coursde cette negociation en aucune circonstance en dehors du contexte de celle-ci.
5 les deux parties sont d'accord pour qu'il n'y ait pas de declarations ou fuites ci la presse sur le contenu des negociations, cimoins qu'elles n'en decident autrement d'un commun accord.
6 Les deux parties s'engagent ci s'abstenir de toute initiative ou ac te relatifs au plateau continental de la rner Egee qui pourrait gener la negociation.
7 Les deux parties s'engagent, en ce qui concerne leurs relations bilaterales, ci s'abstenir de toute initiative ou acte qui tendrait a discrediter I' autre.
8 Les deux parties se so nt rnises d'accord d'etudier la pratique des etats et les regles internationales en cette matiere, en vue d'en degager certains principes et criteres pratiques qui pourraient servir dans le cas de la delimitation du plateau continental entre les deux pays.
9 A cet effet, une commission mixte sera creee, qui sera compo-" see par des representants nationaux.
10 Les deux parties acceptent d'adopter un rythme graduel dans le processus de la negociation ci suivre, apres consultation entre elles.

Quoted from *Athens News Agency,* 28 March 1987.

2 *Athens News Agency,* 6 March 1988

3 *Athens News Agency*, 7. März 1988.

very country that had occupied Cyprus for 13 years and constantly threatened Greece's integrity should accuse Greece of expansionism.[1]

On 11 March, the conflict took on another dimension. On that day, Foreign Minister Papoulias called the American ambassador in Athens, Robert Keeley, to the ministry to complain about recent statements by some members of the US government. This was preceded, as already mentioned, by the Reagan administration's attempt to override the 7:10 ratio.

On 19 February, the member of the House of Representatives, Gus Yatron, who was also the Chairman of the Subcommittee on Human Rights of the House Committee on Foreign Affairs, informed Secretary of Defence Weinberger that he had submitted to Congress an amendment to the Foreign Aid Bill for the fiscal year 1988. This amendment was to prohibit the use in Cyprus of military aid received by Turkey from the USA. Weinberger was asked to explain to him how the use of such material by the Turkish occupation forces in Cyprus could be justified, since the aid supplies were only intended for defence purposes.

Weinberger replied that he was only aware that Turkey had replaced some obsolete tanks with more modern ones in Cyprus. This does not' violate US law. A violation of the law would only occur if these weapons were used for offensive purposes.

Weinberger then went into the strategic importance of Turkey. It lies at the intersection of various regional strategies of the USA. Of all the allies, only Turkey had a longer border with the Soviet Union, and in the east and south it bordered politically unstable countries. In addition, Turkey plans its defence extremely efficiently.

Gus Yatron countered: The Reagan administration is guided only by military considerations. For example, it simply did not take note of the annual State of Human Rights report recently published by the State Department, which accused Turkey of massive violations of human rights.[2]

Athens and Nicosia expressed displeasure at Weinberger's remarks. The Cypriot government spokesman, Petros Voskaridis, accused the US of supporting the Turkish occupation forces.[3] On 25 February, US Secretary of State Shultz tried to soften the impact of Weinberger's remarks at a hearing before the same House committee. Nevertheless, on the same day Athens announced that the planned US trip of the Greek deputy prime minister and defence minister, Charalambopoulos would be postponed. It was clear that this was a reaction to Weinberger's statements.

On 4 March, US Secretary of State Rozanne Ridgway and Secretary of Defence Richard Perle testified before the House Foreign Affairs Committee. Perle argued that the 7:1 arrangement was obsolete; US aid to Turkey had to be tripled because, unlike Greece, it had no additional funds. The balance of power must be maintained. Rozanne Ridgway expressed a similar view, emphasising in particular the alleged balance of power in Cyprus.[4]

Athens was so outraged by these remarks, made at a time of growing tensions with Turkey, that on 5 March it cancelled Weinberger's long-planned visit for the second half of March. Weinberger was planning to visit both Athens and Ankara at that time. On 6 March, the Greek ambassador in Washington officially protested against the statements of Ridgway and Perle: the 7:10 relationship had been established by treaty since the Greek-American Defence and

1 *Athens News Agency,* 10 March 1988.
2 *Athens News Agency,* 20 February 1987.
3 *Athens News Agency,* 21 February 1987
4 *Athens News Agency,* 5 March 1987. She gave the following figures: Turkish troops in Cyprus 22,000 -30,000, Turkish Cypriot National Guard 4,500, Cypriot National Guard 12,000-13,000, National Guard reserves 30,000, 1,300 Greek troops, and a larger number of Greek officers serving in the National Guard.

Economic Cooperation Agreement of 1983. The new proposals of the administration were unacceptable and damaged the climate of Greek-American relations. Moreover, Perle's statement would lead to a strengthening of Turkish intransigence and provocativeness.[1]

On 7 March, Papandreou criticised the US position before a PASOK party event. He said that the administration should make a course correction, which was the only way to improve bilateral relations. The USA regarded Turkey as a kind of substitute for Iran, as a kind of regional policeman who was to look after US interests in the Middle East. In doing so, the USA overlooks the fact that Turkey is striving towards the West and aims at the Aegean and Cyprus. He was ready for talks, but dialogue was a matter of give and take, and since Greece made no demands, little positive could come out of such a dialogue.[2]

On 10 March, the Athens government spokesperson stated that the 7:10 ratio was and hopefully would remain a treaty obligation. On 11 March, as mentioned above, the Greek Foreign Ministry lodged an official protest against another statement by the Director of the Defence Security Assistance Policy Division at the US Department of Defence, Lieutenant General Philip Gast. On 10 March, Gast had repeated Weinberger's statement to the Senate Foreign Relations Committee that Turkish troops in Cyprus were only there for defence purposes. Senator Paul Simon had then stated that the Pentagon was obviously favouring Turkey for strategic reasons.

On 12 March, Foreign Minister Papoulias told US Ambassador Keeley that maintaining the 7:10 ratio and the balance of power was a conditio sine qua non. At the same time, the Greek Cypriot pressure group in Washington raised massive accusations against Turkey at various hearings. On the same day, Secretary of State .Firle resigned from his office "for personal reasons". The next day (13 March) it became known in Washington that the State Department considered Einberger's and Perle's statements to be extremely unproductive and to exceed their authority.[3]

Prime Minister Özal, who was still convalescing in Houston, obviously relied on the Pentagon when he stated that the problems between Greece and Turkey could only be solved by Turkey becoming stronger: "The only thing that can force the Greeks to agree is a strong Turkey. He then suspected the Greek government of having authorised the activities of the NAPC.[4] Foreign Minister Halefoglou rejected the Greek accusations and referred to the 1976 Security Council resolution that had called on both sides to reduce their tensions in the Aegean. Finally, on 15 March, State Department spokesman Charles Redman attempted to defuse relations between Athens and Washington by stating, among other things, that the US would welcome a withdrawal of all non-Cypriot troops from the island as part of a solution to the Cyprus problem. Clearly, the State Department was trying to regain the initiative on this issue.

16 March saw three contrasting developments: In Athens, Papandreou and Kyprianou conferred and discussed short-, medium- and long-term problems, noting a broad congruence of views. In Brussels, Secretary of State Pangalos declined to discuss Turkey's possible application for EC membership. At the same time, he submitted a memorandum to the EC Council of Ministers and the Commission, informing both bodies of the economic discrimination against Greeks living in Turkey that had been going on since 1964. Only if these discriminatory laws, which violated international law, were repealed, would Greece sign the so-called

1 *Athens News Agency,* 7 March 1987
2 *Athens News Agency,* 9. März 1987.
3 *Athens News Agency,* 14 March 1987 on the basis of a dpa report.
4 *Athens News Agency.* 14 March 1987: "The only thing that can force the Greeks to reach an agreement is a strong Turkey" .

Adaptation Agreement to the Turkish Association Agreement with the EC [1] In Washington, an agreement between the USA and Turkey on defence and economic cooperation was initialled for a period of five years.

This agreement was, to put it mildly, somewhat extraordinary. It was signed at a time when the mood in Congress was more than negative for a change in the 7: 10 ratio. Secretary of State Shultz's accompanying letter gave assurances that the administration would try to push through as much aid to Turkey as possible. The New York Times was sure that Congress would view the administration's role as a Turkish lobby with displeasure. The whole affair, it said, was only provoking Congress.

Promptly, on 17 March, the House Subcommittee for Europe extended the validity of the 7:10 rule to the supply of military surplus material. An amendment even proposed that aid to Turkey should be reduced if it did not reduce the number of its troops stationed in Cyprus. At the same time, the committee cut the planned aid by a quarter, proposing $343 million for Greece and $490 million for Turkey for 1988. Defence Minister Weinberger, who had arrived in Ankara in the meantime, said that he would do everything to prevent cuts by Congress.

Meanwhile, the exchange of statements between Athens and Ankara continued. On 18 March, Foreign Minister Halefoglou predicted a "hot summer" if Greece did not change its position. Athens announced that it would not be impressed by threatening statements.[2] On 19 March, in Houston, Özal indicated that he regarded Greek-Turkish relations as a kind of game. In Ankara, Hasan Cemal Güzel, Minister of State in the Prime Minister's Office, said that Greece had always been a threat to Turkey, but that they were ready to meet any threat in the Aegean. The Turkish Foreign Ministry protested to the Greek ambassador against the constant "hunting" of the Piri Reis by the Greek air force. In Washington, Halefoglou called on the US administration to enforce its commitments in the defence agreement in Congress.[3] A day later, in a speech at the Brookings Research Institute in Washington, Halefoglou said that if Greece continued to violate the Berne Declaration, Turkey would take the necessary measures.[4]

On 20 March, Athens responded with a demarche to the Turkish ambassador in Athens: the presence of the Piri Reis was a provocation. It was accompanied by two warships, was outside Greek territorial waters, but had carried out research without informing Athens in an area which, according to international law, belonged to Greece. Greece would take all necessary measures and rejected any responsibility for unforeseen consequences. The NATO and EC ambassadors had been informed of this.[5]

In Washington, the confrontation between the administration and Congress also continued. Secretary of State Derwinski told another House subcommittee that the Greeks were exaggerating the importance of the modernisation of Turkish weapons in Cyprus and that Turkish troops there posed no threat to Greek Cypriots. This statement in turn prompted congressmen and senators to take an even tougher stance. When it became known that the administration wanted to undermine the Congressional cuts by supplying material, voices were even raised in Congress demanding a 1:1 ratio.[6]

On 21 March, the Ministers of Defence and Foreign Affairs (Charalambopoulos and Papoulias) and the Greek Chief of Staff (Air Force General Nikos Kouris) met in Athens under

---

1 *Athens News Agency,* 17 March 1987.
2 *Athens News Agency,* 20 March 1987.
3 Ibidem
4 *Athens News Agency,* 21. March 1987
5 *Athens News Agency,* 23. March 1987. "We don't want any difficulties. Both sides have to be careful and I recommend special caution to the Greeks".
6 *Athens News Agency,* 23. März 1987.

the chairmanship of Papandreou and discussed the situation. It was decided to inform US Secretary of State Shultz and NATO Secretary General Lord Carrington that Greece would no longer tolerate actions like those of the Piri Reis and would take measures to defend its sovereignty.[1]

On the same day, Ankara declared that it would continue to do as it pleased in the Aegean. In Houston, Özal stated in a television interview broadcast live to Turkey that Turkey did not want trouble, but he recommended special caution to the Greeks: *"We do not want trouble. Both sides must be careful, and I recommend particuJar care on the part of the Greeks".* [2]

Ex-Secretary of State Perle claimed in an interview with a Turkish newspaper that Özal had tried to melt the ice between Ankara and Athens, but Papandreou had not responded. Athens was preventing the creation of an atmosphere of rapprochement between the two countries and was to blame if no agreement was reached in Cyprus. There will certainly be no war between Greece and Turkey. "He added that he did not think that the Greeks could undertake such a foolish action as extending their territorial waters. Incidents might be created at the border, in the air or on the sea, and were dangerous. But the decision to carry out a military intervention had to be taken by the two capitals and, he said, he did not believe this could happen".[3]

Athens' reaction on 22 March was determined. Government spokesman Roubatis repeated the warning of the 21st and described Perle as a paid employee of Ankara who had always unreservedly taken Ankara's side. Perle should show restraint until he finally leaves office.[4] On 23 March, Athens received the official response from the State Department to the demarche of 12 March, which, however, did not satisfy the Greek government.

During the next two days, Greek politics was absorbed by the preparations for the National Day and largely left the field to Ankara. Although during these days, as before, there were repeated violations of the Athens FIR by Turkish aircraft, Papandreou did not go beyond what he had said earlier in his National Day address: Greece was not prepared to give up its national sovereignty rights under any circumstances; although it did not want to, it was prepared to fight for it.

On 23 March, Turkey's UN Ambassador, Turkmen, delivered a letter to Perez de Cuellar and the Security Council claiming that the planned Greek oil drilling was a breach of the Berne Declaration. Turkey would not accept any unilateral action by Greece with regard to the shelf. A day later, the Secretary of State in the Turkish Foreign Ministry, Nuzet Kandemir, summoned the ambassadors of the NATO and EC countries and accused Greece of creating faits accomplis to serve its expansionist aims. March 25 saw maximum activity on the Turkish side. In Houston, Özal repeated his call for a dialogue. In Ankara, the National Security Council met and called on the government to take the necessary measures. Subsequently, Minister of State Güzel informed Özal of the decisions taken.

---

1 *Athens News Agency*, 23. März 1987.
"We don't want any difficulties. Both sides have to be careful and I recommend special caution to the Greeks".

2 *Athens News Agency,* 23. März 1987.
"He added that he did not think the Greeks could do something as crazy as extend their territorial waters. There could be incidents at the border. in the air and at sea. These are certainly dangerous, but the decision to launch a military intervention must be taken in the capitals and he does not believe that this can happen".

3 *ibidem.*

4 A copy of the map can be found in *Spotlight,* Nr. 50 (March 1987), p. 10.

Ankara's provocative attitude began to worry international politics. In Brussels, NATO Secretary General Carrington expressed his deep concern about the escalation of tensions and the deterioration of relations between Greece and Turkey. A group of 10 US senators called on Secretary of State Shultz to convey their deep unease about the situation to Özal.

The measures adopted by the Turkish National Security Council turned out to be a copy of the 1976 action that had almost led to war at the time.

On 26 March, Ankara published the text of the letter to the UN Security Council. At the same time, it became known that the government had granted the state oil company TPAO exploration and drilling licences in the Aegean Sea near Samothrace, Limnos and Lesvos. In the government gazette of 25 March, a map was printed that bore a fatal resemblance to the one of 1974:[1] 95 per cent of the areas marked there concerned the Greek shelf. Minister of State Güzel added that the Sismik 1(the Piri Reis had in the meantime entered a port in the Dardanelles for repairs) had started moving towards the Aegean and would operate there until Ankara's economic and political goals were achieved. He hoped that Greece would not hinder the work of Sismik 1, but if it did, all necessary measures would be taken, not even excluding the use of the Turkish fleet.[2]

On the same day, Özal arrived in London on his return flight from Houston. After a conversation with the British Foreign Secretary, Geoffrey Howe, he assured that his country had only friendly intentions towards Greece. He then accused Papandreou of playing up the current crisis for domestic political reasons. Greece should abide by the Berne Declaration. The opening of a dialogue was urgently needed.

In Athens, following a meeting of the National Defence Council (KYSEA), the government spokesperson stated that the necessary measures would be taken should Sismik 1 begin seismic surveys. At the same time, the Athens Foreign Ministry, through the Turkish Ambassador in Athens, Akiman, asked Ankara to submit the shelf issue to the International Court of Justice.

On 27 March, Papandreou briefed the full cabinet in detail on the situation.[3] Summing up, he stated that the National Defence Council (KYSEA) had decided not to let Sismik 1 carry out seismic measurements. Turkey is reportedly seeking dialogue. He said there was only one thing on which dialogue could be held: on the formulation of a joint application on the delimitation of the shelf to the International Court of Justice. The issue is "legal delimitation", not "political distribution". He said he was ready to start dialogue with Turkey on legal issues, but not on political ones. Should war break out over Sismik 1, he said, this would lead to radical changes in the entire Balkan region, which would also affect NATO.

Papandreou then pointed to the fact that Özal and Halefoglou were in the USA and Weinberger and Perle were in Turkey. Without elaborating on this, Papandreou stressed that if this was an attempt by NATO or the US to force Greece to negotiate with Turkey on all issues, the Greek government would not accept it. Foreign Minister Papoulias would inform the Bulgarian government today in accordance with the non-aggression pact.[4]

In the subsequent press conference, Papandreou was even more explicit: one would not prevent the activities of Sismik 1 with words. Should a conflict arise, the US bases in Greece would also be closed.

---

1 *Athens News Agency,* 27. März 1987.

2 Text of the speech in *Athens News Agency,* 28. März 1987.

3 Full text of Prime minister Andreas Papandreou's speech to the Cabinet on Friday 27 March 1987 in Feature Stories, *Athens News Agency,* 28 March: 1987.

4 The text of the letter was published on 28 March. *Athens News Agency,* 28 March 1987.

Later in the day, Foreign Minister Papoulias flew to Sofia to deliver a personal message from Papandreou to Todor Shifkoff about the situation. Secretary of State Kapsis asked US Ambassador Keeley to suspend operations at the Nea Makri communications base near Athens in accordance with Article 7 of the Greek-US base agreement. After completing his lightning visit to Sofia, Papoulias briefed the ambassadors of the Warsaw Pact countries, Yugoslavia and the Islamic countries on the situation. Only afterwards did State Secretary Kapsis inform the ambassadors of the NATO countries, which caused considerable irritation in NATO circles.

In New York, UN Ambassador Dountas presented the UN Secretary-General with a response[1] to the Turkish letter of 23 March, which stated, among other things, that the drilling projects had been announced by NAPC, but that the Greek government had expressly forbidden them. The Turkish government had been informed of this. Perez de Cuellar expressed his deep concern.

In Ankara, a military spokesperson announced that the Sismik 1 would leave for the Aegean the following day under military protection. Should the Sismik t be obstructed, countermeasures would be taken without hesitation. The Turkish armed forces along the Evros border, the Aegean coast and in Northern Cyprus had been put on alert. However, no mobilisation has been ordered.

The Turkish Foreign Ministry tried to divert attention from the renewed Greek proposal to bring the Shelf issue to the International Court of Justice by diplomatic manoeuvres. The ministry's spokesman, Yalim Eralp, said that at this stage Turkey did not intend to go to the Hague. Instead, the conflict should be resolved through direct negotiations on the basis of Security Council Resolution 395 of 1976.

Turkish politicians reacted differently. Former Prime Minister Demirel advised both sides to keep a cool head; the differences could be settled through negotiations. The leader of the Socialist People's Democratic Party, Erdal Inönü, called on the Turkish government to take a hard line. Deputy Prime Minister Kaya Erdem said that as long as no agreement was reached on the demarcation line of the shelf, both states would have equal rights. Turkey was forced to respond to Greece with the same means.

In Brussels, NATO Secretary General Carrington offered his mediation services. When it became known that both Greece and Turkey had imposed holiday closures and launched their war fleets into the Aegean, a meeting of NATO ambassadors was convened, expressing concern and appealing to both sides to refrain from the use of force.

---

1 Ronald Meinardus, "Eine neue Phase in den griechisch-türkischen Beziehungen", *Europa Archiv,* 43: 14 (July 1988), p.405.

In Washington, State Department spokesman Charles Redman announced that the USA had urged both sides to exercise restraint. They are in contact with both sides and are trying to find ways to reduce tensions. The meeting of NATO ambassadors in Brussels was only one attempt to do so. In addition, efforts are being made to obtain precise information on the causes of the crisis.

The British and US ambassadors turned to the Turkish Foreign Office and urged diplomats to de-escalate the crisis. In London, the Foreign Office conveyed the deep concern of the allies to Prime Minister Özal. The pressure on the Turkish leadership from all sides had an effect. In London, Prime Minister Özal told the Anatolia News Agency that he saw no reason to escalate the crisis. However, he declined to comment further for the time being. Later, in an interview with Turkish Radio, he added that if the Greeks did not explore outside their territorial waters, Turkey would not do so either. A report from Ankara by the REUTERS news agency said Özal had also announced that the Sismik 1 would not enter the disputed waters. This defused the crisis.

On 28 March, the de-escalation process was initiated. The NAPC announced that it would refrain from drilling outside Greek territorial waters. This statement was immediately taken up by the Turkish Foreign Ministry and used as a "face-saving" justification for the change of course. The Sismik 1 did leave, but remained in Turkish territorial waters and had no military escort.

The Greek government offered Ankara dialogue on the formulation of a compromise for a joint passage to the Hague. At the same time, it lifted the ban on the American Nea Makri base. In the afternoon, Foreign Minister Papoulias arrived in Washington. Talks followed with Secretary of State Ridgway and officials of the State Department's Southern Europe Division, in which Papoulias informed the. Americans in detail about the developments of the past few days. In Brussels, NATO Secretary General Carrington complained in a BBC interview that neither Greece nor Turkey had made use of his good offices. He was particularly annoyed by a remark made by Özal that he should have intervened earlier. Özal then relented and asked Carrington to mediate.

On the same day, initial talks took place in Brussels between the Turkish Minister of State for EC Affairs, Ali Bozer, and the EC Commissioner for Mediterranean Affairs, Claude Cheysson. Bozer stated that Turkey would apply for Voluntary Membership in the near future. Cheysson gave him to understand that the crisis had not made Ankara's way into the EC any easier. Bozer, on the other hand, put forward an argument that was to become a standard Turkish argument within a short time: It was precisely EC accession that would defuse the Greek-Turkish conflict.

On 29 March, Özal returned to Ankara, where he was greeted with jubilation by his supporters. In Athens, Papandreou received the Turkish ambassador Nazmi Akiman for the first time since he took office in 1984. Akiman delivered to him a position paper by Özal, which the latter had formulated while still in London. Papandreou gave him a message to Prime Minister Özal, which Akiman delivered in Ankara on 30 March. At a subsequent press conference, Özal stated that the differences with Greece should be settled peacefully and that he was satisfied with Papandreou's message. Although there would be no Greek-Turkish summit for the time being, he said he was optimistic about the start of dialogue. Both sides should make every effort to resolve their differences peacefully.

Without straining historical interpretation, the beginning of the Turkish-Greek dialogue can be dated to this first exchange of messages. At the same time, it was a return to the policy of the Berne Declaration of 1976, to a policy of quid pro quo.[1]

The opposition in Ankara was less satisfied. The leader of the Socialist People's Democratic Party, Erdal Inönü, criticised that it was against Turkish interest to bring the Aegean conflict before the International Court of Justice. Bülent Ecevit accused Özal of going along with the Greek course, saying that Turkey was not bound by the Berne Declaration because Athens was violating it. Demirel suspected that Özal's change of course had come about under NATO pressure. President Kenan Evren, however, welcomed the start of the dialogue.

In Washington, too, efforts were made to improve relations with Athens. Secretary of State Shultz and Secretary of State Rozanne Ridgway appeared at the launch of the Onassis Centre for Hellenic Studies at New York University on 30 March. It was quite obvious that Shultz was trying to regain influence over US-Greek relations, which had been mainly controlled by the Pentagon for the past few years.

On 1 April, Ambassador Akiman handed Papandreou a written reply from Özal. Meanwhile, it became known in Ankara that most officials in the Turkish Foreign Ministry had been taken completely by surprise by Özal's action. The diplomatic establishment in Ankara was busy trying to keep Özal's initiative within the limits that could be considered tolerable for the established Turkish Aegean policy. Newspaper commentators, who normally reflect the opinion of the diplomatic establishment, strongly criticised Özal.[2]

On 8 April, Papandreou handed Akiman the Greek government's response. The next day, government spokesman Roubatis noted that strict confidentiality had been agreed. Papandreou rejected secret diplomacy, but the worst that could happen would be if these first tentative steps~ towards each other were led by the Turkish or Greek press. Although it was stated in Athens that the topic of the dialogue was the joint march to The Hague, it became known in Ankara that other topics had been raised. On 10 April, Özal stated on Turkish television that the Aegean problem also had a legal side.

Over the next few months, the situation eased. Athens took control of the NAPC and did not authorise any new drilling attempts outside Greek territorial waters, although it reserved the right to do so. Ankara also held back. Thus, in the end, the situation of the Berne Declaration of 1976 had been reached again. In the USA, the Greek Cypriot lobby in Congress pushed through the maintenance of the 7:10 ratio. The only difference to the status quo ante was that the dialogue by letter between Papandreou and Özal continued.

Almost nothing about the content of this correspondence was made public. Both sides maintained absolute confidentiality. To all appearances, the dialogue expanded in the course of time. While at the beginning the Greek side only spoke of negotiating a compromise, of determining the modalities of a joint appeal to the International Court of Justice[3] the further development suggests that the dialogue later turned to more comprehensive topics.

In the course of the summer and autumn, more shrill tones were heard from Ankara, but these were connected with the pre-election campaign in Turkey and were received calmly in Athens. On 18 August, Özal addressed the situation of the Turkish minority in Bulgaria and announced that the issue would be settled there sooner or later, similar to what had happened in Cyprus. On 23 August, he stated that the Turkish army was getting stronger and the

---

1 *Athens News Agency,* 4 April 1987.

2 Meinardus, *op.cit.,* p. 93.

3 Greece. Background *-News -Information,* Nr. 22 (24. September 1987).

Bulgarians and Greeks were afraid of it.[1] In September, the almost obligatory Greek protests took place during the annual NATO exercise "Display Determination 87". Defence Minister Charalambopoulos even said that the NATO exercise indirectly served Turkey's expansionist aims and increased rather than reduced tensions in the Aegean. But it was obvious that neither side took these statements seriously. On 2 October, Özal informed Papandreou that the dialogue could only continue after the elections at the end of November 1987.

The Development of the Cyprus Question from October 1986 to the End of 1987

Compared to the Greek-Turkish storms over the Aegean, the political weather situation in Cyprus during this period was almost calm. In broad outline, the development can be sketched as follows.

The Cypriot government continued to seek international support after the Non-Aligned Conference. In particular, it repeatedly pointed to the increase in Turkish troops, estimated at 36,000 in October 1986, and the increase in settlers (65,000 at the same time). In November 1986, Perez de Cuellar's representative, Marrack Goulding, and another UN representative arrived in Cyprus for exploratory talks. In December, Cyprus' UN ambassador to the Security Council called for the withdrawal of all foreign troops as a precondition for a settlement. In January 1987, President Kyprianou called for the return of all refugees as a sine qua non for the solution of the Cyprus problem. The problem of the Greek Cypriots missing since 1974 was referred to on several occasions.

UN Secretary General Perez de Cuellar sought to break the deadlock by announcing in January 1987 that he would launch a new Cyprus initiative. In the same month, State Department Special Envoy James Wilkinson sounded out the situation in Cyprus, indicating that the US refused to convene an international conference. In contrast, the Soviet Special Representative, Nikolai Rodionov reiterated the January 1986 proposal and called for intensification of the UN Secretary General's efforts. In March, Perez de Cuellar's Special Representative appeared for confidential talks with the sides in Cyprus. While the Cypriot government maintained confidentiality, Denktash went public. He announced that negotiations would only begin if the Cypriot government first accepted the Draft Framework Agreement of March 1986, behaviour which suggests that Denktash had little interest in a settlement. Perez de Cuellar came to a similar conclusion in his biannual report to the Security Council at the beginning of June: although he would not allow his efforts to fail, he had to note a deterioration of the situation. Mutual mistrust had grown, he said, especially due to the potentially dangerous strengthening of Turkish troops in the north.

Although Nicosia managed to continue collecting declarations of solidarity, they ultimately remained paper declarations and contributed little or nothing to solving the problem. The only substantial progress that could contribute to a solution in the medium term was the rapprochement with the EC: at the end of March it became known that the negotiations between the EC and Cyprus on the conclusion of a customs union were nearing their end. The treaty was signed in mid-October and entered into force in December 1987.

At the end of August it became apparent that the Cyprus issue was further away from a solution than ever. President Kyprianou was obviously aware of this when he announced on 31 August that he intended to initiate a Cyprus debate in the UN General Assembly (the first since 1983). The developments of the past 13 years had shown that a solution could only be found within the framework of an international conference. He then listed the three essentials

1 Uulusal Birlik Partisi or National Unity Party.

for a solution to the problem: withdrawal of Turkish troops and settlers, effective international guarantees and the safeguarding of fundamental freedoms and human rights. Perez de Cuellar stated at the beginning of September that the Cyprus issue was at an impasse: if the existing trend continued, serious confrontations could not be ruled out in the coming months.

On 9 October, Kyprianou presented his position to the UN General Assembly. He reiterated the "essentials" and stressed the Cypriot government's willingness to cooperate with the UN, but at the same time he called for the convening of the international conference that could solve the external aspects of the problem. Ankara must be made to respect UN resolutions, he said. Then Kyprianou went a step further. He offered the total demilitarisation of Cyprus: If Turkish troops and settlers withdrew, he said, he was ready to disband the Cypriot National Guard. Order would then be maintained by an international peacekeeping force paid for by Greece and Cyprus.

This appearance by Kyprianou before the UN General Assembly was the last foreign policy initiative before the Cypriot presidential elections scheduled for February 1988. Before continuing with the account of developments, it seems useful to take a brief look at the internal Cypriot situation at the end of 1987.

Of primary interest here is how the problem of the island was viewed internally at that time, both in the south and in the north, and again not the respective official view of those in power, which was sufficiently well known from numerous announcements. Far more interesting are "off-the-record" remarks by leading politicians or statements by members of the opposition.

Simplistically, one could state the following for the South. There was widespread disillusionment about possible solutions within the UN framework. So many resolutions had been passed that "you could wallpaper the walls of the presidential palace with them", but no solution had been found. An international conference would have a better chance, but the two superpowers would have to agree first. Greater hopes were placed on the EC after the entry into force of the Customs Union, although politicians were rather sceptical.

There was a subliminal feeling of frustration and paralysing powerlessness. At the same time, those in power were afraid of making wrong decisions that could have fatal consequences and jeopardise Makarios' legacy. One got the impression that this was one of the reasons why they stuck rigidly to the previous "'tried and tested" procedure.

But there were also encouraging signs. Obviously, the years of fear of the Turkish army had initiated a process of rethinking. Their own fear enabled some Greek Cypriot politicians to develop understanding for the present and past fears of Turkish Cypriots. A former leading EOKA cadre was self-critical about the past: the EOKA outrages against the Turkish Cypriots were the result of deep blindness and were unforgivable.

The extent of the rethinking process was shown by critical statements about the policy of Makarios, who until then had been "taboo": Makarios' anti-Turkish minority policy in the mid-1960s had been a mistake and had contributed to deepening the inner-Cypriot division. One could well imagine the fears the Turkish Cypriots had suffered. Since one could empathise with their fears, one understood the Turkish Cypriots' need for security and was prepared to accommodate them as far as possible. Provided, of course, that the other side acts in the same way.

The withdrawal of Turkish troops was considered a sine qua non. On the question of the withdrawal of the Turkish settlers, however, there were differing views, ranging from withdrawal to leaving it. A leading conservative politician was of the opinion that the settlers should remain in Cyprus. Cyprus had become home for the growing second generation of Turkish settlers. While further immigration must be stopped, reunification of the island should not be attempted on the basis of a new expulsion. The integration power of the Cypriots is great enough to assimilate the settlers.

Finally, there was a remarkable change in political terminology. Where once there was talk of (Greek) majority and (Turkish) minority, there was now talk of partnership, second nation and equality. This, too, may be seen as a symptom of the profound process of rethinking.

As reasonable and encouraging as these views seemed, however, there was doubt as to whether the older generation of Greek Cypriot politicians would have the strength and courage to translate their views into practical policies. This obviously required a generational change in leadership.

In the north of the island, the rethinking process had only begun among the opposition. The older generation around Denktash and his party supporters were far from understanding the Greek fears. At least outwardly they were of the opinion that because of the past (the 1960s) only the Turkish Cypriots had reason to fear. Greek fears of the Turkish army were rejected as unfounded; the Turkish army posed no threat. On the contrary, only the presence of the Turkish army would eliminate the island Turks' fear of the Greek threat. In general, the concern about the Greek threat was played to the fore by the official side, whereby they did not even shy away from invoking the "Megali Idea", which had long since become history, in the official propaganda. A more than idiosyncratic interpretation of history dates the division of the island not to the year of the proclamation of the "Turkish Republic of Northern Cyprus" or to the year 1974, but to the beginning of the inner-Cypriot conflict in the mid-1960s; at that time Makarios had divided the island.

With a little dialectical acrobatics, a continuing Greek-Cypriot aggression was even constructed. The non-recognition of the North as a separate state was an act of aggression and discrimination in which the whole world participated. The North was the victim of the South. This thesis was underpinned by "human touch stories" designed to appeal to the emotions of the less informed.

From all this, one got the impression that the group around Denktash did not think in the least about approaching the Greek Cypriot side in any way: Their aim, as will be shown in connection with further historical developments, was quite obviously to maintain the status quo. Their attitude to the question of the settlers also spoke for this. They wanted to increase their numbers. Superficially, this is about maintaining power for the Denktash group. Without the votes of the Settlers' Party (YDP/NBP) Denktash would not have been elected "head of state" in 1985. The longer-term goal seemed to be to bring the strength of the island Turks to par with the number of island Greeks. An alienation of the north caused by the influx of Anatolian Turks was denied. In view of this attitude, it is permissible to call the Denktash group the faction of the "concrete heads".

The opposition in the north consists of three parties. Before describing the politics of these parties, it seems useful to make some basic remarks about the Turkish Cypriot parties. With the exception of Özgür's party, all the parties in the north are patronage parties and not programme parties. The clientele character is, of course, most pronounced in Denktash's National Unity Party (UBP/NUP), since its leader has the most opportunities to do "favours" for his supporters. Accordingly, the ideological classifications of the parties should be done with restraint and considered valid only for the moment. The political position of the Turkish Cypriot parties is thus extremely incoherent and inconsistent and ultimately dependent on the day-to-day political decisions of the party leader

The largest opposition party is Özker Özgür's Republican Turkish Party (CTP/RTP)161 . It currently has 12 MPs in parliament and represents a socialist position. The Municipal Liberation Party (TKP/CLP)162 led by the mayor of North Nicosia, Mustafa Akinci, is represented in parliament with 9 MPs. It sees itself as a moderate left-wing party, although its political pendulum can sometimes swing to the right over the centre, depending on expediency. The "left-liberal" Democratic People's Party (DHP) of Ismet Kotak is not represented in parliament, but has some influence on public opinion in the north through the newspaper Kibris Postasi, published by its chairman.

All three parties are extremely critical of the course steered by Denktash. Özgür's criticism is the most pronounced. It is directed against Denktash's domestic policy as well as against his foreign policy course. With regard to domestic policy, Özgür complains above all about Denktash's increasingly authoritarian style of government. Even the proclamation of the republic was an act of political blackmail: When the opposition hesitated to support this serious step, Denktash threatened to ban the opposition parties; the result was the "no" vote in parliament.

According to Özgur, the constitution introduced in 1983 is a copy of Turkey's undemocratic constitution. Democracy in the north is only a sham. Whoever opposes Denktash's course must expect severe repression. Human rights are disregarded. According to Article 10 of the constitution, the Turkish army is responsible for the internal and external security of the north. For example, the police in the north are under the command of the Turkish military commander in Cyprus and the commander of the Turkish Cypriot National Guard is appointed by Ankara.

According to Özgür, Denktash's immigration policy is disastrous. The influx of immigrants continues, so that there is already one immigrant for every two island Turks. What is particularly worrying, he said, is that a veritable exodus of island Turks has begun. The recently concluded labour agreement allows entrepreneurs from the mainland to import their own workers. Upon application, they can stay in Cyprus and become citizens. If this trend continues, "*we fear that the Turkish Cypriots will be outnumbered and their identity as a more cultured and advanced political entity, completely destroyed*".[1]

In a conversation with the author, Özgür categorically demanded the withdrawal of the Turkish settlers. Although the government is trying to make the immigrants citizens, they are not ready to become Cypriots. Even the second generation perceives itself as Turkish and not as Turkish-Cypriot. The immigrants live in their special villages and have hardly any contact with the Turkish Cypriots. In the schools of the Turkish villages, a Turkish, but not a Turkish-Cypriot national feeling is conveyed. In addition, the Turkish immigrants are unfamiliar with family planning. How little the immigrants identify with Cyprus is also shown by the fact that they do not reinvest their money earned in Cyprus in the country, but transfer it back to their actual homeland. It seems that the immigrants have a mentality similar to that of the "guest workers" in Western Europe.

Unfortunately, in the north as well as in the south of Cyprus, the hardliners were in charge. Although the agreements of 1977 and 1979 provided for the normalisation of the situation on the island, contacts between the people of the two parts were forbidden. In recent years, almost nothing has happened to contribute to reconciliation. Both sides talk about reunifica-

---

1 Republican Turkish Party, *Speech delivered by Özker Özgüt. President of the Turkish Republican Party, at the seminar on the Turco-Greelf disputes, held in Munich. between 29th-31st January, 1988.*
"We fear that Turkish Cypriots will become a minority and the identity of their culturally and politically more developed society will be completely destroyed".

tion on a federal basis. But: *"So far both sides have paid lip service to this. While spending no effort towards a federal solution, the people themselves are not being given the chance to prepare for a federal get-together. The process of integration of the North into Turkey is continuing and if it is not stopped, in not later than ten years, the demography will have changed in favour of the settlers from the mainland and the idea of a federal Republic will gradually fade away."*.[1]

During the discussion, Özgür expressed great understanding for the fears of the Greek side. It is important to quickly overcome the vicious circle of mutual mistrust. To do this, it is necessary for people to come together again, to work and live together, so that they can trust each other again. The road to reunification must be prepared by a kind of road map. First of all, an agreement had to be reached on the chronological process. Then a provisional government would have to be formed, after which the Turkish troops and possibly all other troops would have to leave the country. Denktash's demand for prior recognition of the north as a state would only deepen the division and reduce the chances of a solution. Greek and Turkish Cypriots would have to have equal rights in the future state, but not in the sense of artificial quotas as in the past, but by understanding and respecting each other as two peoples in one state.

A comparison of the two "unofficial" positions in the South and North at the end of 1987 shows that they were very similar. If these forces were to come to the fore in both parts of Cyprus, there would certainly be the possibility of initiating a new policy.

At the end of 1987, the following possibility emerged. Should there be a generational change in the elections in the south, and should the opposition parties succeed in uniting in the next parliamentary elections in the north (probably in 1989) (for which there were beginnings at the end of 1987), there could be a change of power in the government in the north. Although Denktash would continue to serve as 'president', a government based on the opposition would certainly push for the resumption of intercommunal talks. Under these conditions, it is conceivable that the inter-communal talks could soon prove fruitful, especially since they would then be led by politicians who felt themselves to be Cypriots.

Should there be no change of power due to the high number of votes of the Settlers' Party, which would in any case support the Denktash faction, there were nevertheless prospects for a possible solution at the end of 1987.

Increasingly, Northern Cyprus had become a burden for Turkey, both economically and politically: Ankara had to contribute about half of the budget of the "Turkish Republic of Northern Cyprus". When these "aid payments", including borrowing, reached around $60 million in the 1987 financial year, Ankara made it clear to Denktash that things could not go on like this. Özal indicated that Turkey would gradually reduce the subsidies and stop them altogether from 1992. From then on there would only be project-related aid payments.

However, such a measure would hit the Denktash regime hard. The bulk of Turkish aid payments have so far gone into the pockets of state employees, who make up the majority of the workforce in the north. Three quarters of the industry in the north[2] and as much as 80 per cent of the hotels in the north are state-owned , and both sectors are running high deficits. If

---

1 *ibidem.*
"So far, both sides have only talked about it. Nothing is being done to reach a federal solution and the people themselves are being denied the opportunity to prepare for federal cooperation. The process of integrating the north into Turkey continues, and if it is not stopped, in ten years at the latest the demography will have changed in favour of the settlers from the mainland and the idea of a federal republic will slowly disappear."

2 Gerd Höhler in *Frankfurter Rundschau* am 15 December 1986.

Ankara were to actually impose an austerity programme on the North, this would almost certainly mean a political weakening of the Denktash faction, which would manifest itself in the 1989 elections: it is very unlikely that those affected by the austerity programme would continue to vote for Denktash's party.

Politically, too, Northern Cyprus is increasingly becoming a burden for Turkey. Although Ankara cared quite little about the frequent condemnations in the UN, Özal obviously understood that even starting a discussion on Turkey's possible EC accession was out of the question before the Cyprus question (and the Aegean conflict) was solved. Therefore, in his last letter to Papandreou before the Turkish elections of 29 November 1987, he proposed a meeting.

The Davos Meeting

On election night, Papandreou did not rule out such a meeting. Two days later, he congratulated Özal on his re-election and expressed his hope that their contact would continue for the benefit of both countries. Özal welcomed this message. He hoped that their dialogue would open the way to cooperation between the two countries. At the same time, however, voices from the Turkish Foreign Ministry countered Özal's conciliatory tones, showing that the Turkish Prime Minister would continue to face stalling resistance from the diplomatic establishment.

On 8 January 1988 it was announced in Athens that Papandreou and Özal would meet in Davos on 30 and 31 January within the framework of the annual World Management Forum. A few weeks later it was learned that the initiative for this had come from Papandreou. In the following days, however, there was a repeated exchange of polemical statements. Nevertheless, on 16 January, Foreign Minister Mesut Yilmaz stated that Ankara had determined its course to be followed in Davos: The aim, he said, was to promote mutual trust. Turkey had not imposed any conditions for meetings, but neither did it accept any. If the withdrawal of Turkish troops from Cyprus is made a precondition for talks, the meeting will be ineffective. The dialogue in Davos would be on innocuous topics such as communication, tourism, trade and joint ventures. At the same time, it became known that Özal was under massive fire from the socialist opposition in parliament, which demanded a foreign policy debate even before the Davos meeting because it wanted to pre-empt possible concessions by Özal. Özal rejected this request.

On 19 January, Özal warned that one should not expect miracles from the Davos meeting. Two months later, in an interview with Cumhurriyet, Özal said that the dialogue should start with simple issues. For example, the problem of the Greek minority in Istanbul could easily be solved. Contacts on a non-official level could also help to reduce hostility. The Greek government did not participate in these "pre-conference statements"; it was obviously trying to play down the importance of the meeting and avoid attacks by the opposition. Any concessions made before the meeting could have easily exposed Papandreou to accusations of "betrayal of the national cause". From this point of view, Özal's statement on the Greek minority was a courageous advance, especially since he too was being watched suspiciously by an extremely aggressive opposition.

It seems that Özal could hardly wait for the meeting with Papandreou. This is the only ex-planation for the fact that he sought a first meeting with his Greek counterpart even before the scheduled date: he spontaneously mingled with the guests at a Greek reception and greeted Papandreou. But the conversation between the two was limited to "small talk."

At the first meeting that followed, however, they very quickly had a frank conversation. Although confidentiality was agreed on the content of the talks, enough details were mentioned at the joint press conference on 31 January for some conclusions to be drawn about the course of the talks.

With the exception of Turkey's accession to the EC, there was practically no issue that was left out of the exchange of views. It was clear to both sides that no concrete solutions would be found and therefore they did not try to find any. Instead, they presented their respective positions and took note of each other's positions without approving them, but also without rejecting them.

With regard to the Aegean, Papandreou proposed going to The Hague together by consensus; Özal expressed his well-known reservations. It was therefore decided to put this problem on ice for the time being, to come back to it in due course. The Cyprus problem was similar: Papandreou stressed that he did not consider it a bilateral problem but an international one, a problem of foreign occupation that had to be solved within the UN. He himself was in favour of the total demilitarisation of the island. The Turkish occupation forces should be withdrawn, the Cypriot National Guard should be dissolved at the same time and replaced by a unified police force that would be financed entirely by the Cypriot government. Özal did not accept this proposal either, but did not reject it either. Then Papandreou raised the problem of the disappearances since 1974. Özal, on the other hand, spoke about the problem of the Greek minority in Istanbul in such an understanding way that the Greek prime minister was more than taken in. The incidents in the Thracian town of Komotini on the day of their arrival in Davos were seen by both premiers as a manoeuvre by interested circles to torpedo their meeting.

Both sides agreed that there should never again be a situation like that of March 1987. They decided that the use of force should be excluded in the pursuit of any solutions. The two premiers were also quite united in their assessment of the international situation. Both firmly rejected any outside interference in their bilateral relations. It was unacceptable that attempts were being made to capitalise on Turkish-Greek differences. Neither Greece nor Turkey was under the curatorship of any great power. It was clear that the Americans were meant.[1]

At the end of their talks, a joint communiqué was published: It read: The Prime Ministers of Greece and Turkey met twice in Davos Switzerland, on 30th -31 st January 1988, and discussed issues of mutual concern in an atmosphere of understanding and good will.

1. *The Prime Ministers observed that accumulated problems created in time due to different approaches are at times exploited by certain circles. It is imperative that this should not be permitted. They agreed that closing the gap between these differences will require time good will and hard work.*
2. *The Prime Ministers gave their views of Turco-Greek relations, starting from a historie perspective ancl their deterioration in time. They further elaborated on the recent crisis in the Aegean which brought the two countries to the brink of war, expressed at the same time their optimism introduced as a consequence of exchange of messages between them. They agreed that from now on such a crisis should never be repeated and both sides must concentrate their efforts for the establishment of lasting peaceful relations.*
3. *The Prime Ministers agreed that rigid frames of mind have been created in various segments of their societies in relation to existing issues. They noted that this is the case even in textbooks. They noted also with regret so me statements of officials not conducive to an improvement of relations between the two countries.*

1 *Spotlight,* Nr. 58, January (1988), p. 2f.

4. *The two Prime Ministers reiterated their perspective positions on issues of bilateral and regional interest.*
5. *They nevertheless underlined that a thaw and a rapprochement between the two countries would require determination, sustained efforts and building of confidence for which the two sides should move to common ground, in order to create an environment conducive to working out lasting solutions.*
6. *The Prime Ministers agreed to establish two committees: one to explore the areas of cooperation such as economic cooperation, joint ventures, trade, tourism, communications, cultural exchanges; and one to define the problem areas, explore the possibilities of closing the gap and nlove towards lasting solutions, the progress of which will be reviewed by the two Prime Ministers. In this regard, they agreed to initiate, encourage and increase contacts among civilian and military officials, members of the press and businessmen, and to establish a Business Council or a Joint Chamber of Commerce and Industry.*
7. *The Prime Ministers also agreed to meet at least once a year and to make reciprocal visits to their countries, and agreed to set up a direct telephone line. They also agreed that the ambassadors of the two countries to international organisations should increase contacts with a view to improving cooperation.*
8. *Finally, both Prime Ministers expressed their satisfaction in the frank and open discussions which took place between themselves, and reiterated their conviction that creation of improved relations and confidence would require resolve, time and hard work."*[1]

The text contained some important new elements: In order to reduce the existing tensions between the two countries, school textbooks should be cleansed of resentment, among other things. Two committees were to be set up. The first, the economic committee, should examine possibilities for cooperation in the economic sector. The task of the second committee would be to draw up an inventory of the problem areas existing between the countries and to examine possible solutions. Both Premiers would closely follow the activities of the committees, i.e. they would supervise their work. A united business committee or a joint chamber of commerce should be established. From now on, the Premiers would meet at least once a year. In order to prevent events like the one in March 1987, a direct telephone connection between them would be established. Military exercises in the Aegean would be announced in advance. Finally, the ambassadors of both countries should maintain contact with international organisations in order to improve cooperation. In conclusion, both Premiers once again expressed their will for peaceful cooperation.

An evaluation of the Davos meeting is difficult in view of the short distance in time. The frequently asked question about the winner of the meeting seems idle. If there was a winner, it was possibly peace in the region. Obviously under the aftermath of the shock of the March 1987 crisis, both sides moved away from their dangerous and unfruitful preconditions for negotiations, while not abandoning their real objectives. The decisive significance of the Davos Summit lies firstly in the fact that both sides decided on a policy of non-war in principle, as Papandreou put it. Secondly, both prime ministers decided on a radical change of priorities: The primary objective is no longer the implementation of the respective major solution.... at the expense of the other, but rather a policy of small steps towards each other, namely the at-

1 Quoted from: *Greece. Background-News-Information,* Nr. 27, 25 February 1988.

tempt to seek solutions where they can easily be found without the opposition in both countries being able to brand the compromise found as national betrayal. On the basis of the trust achieved through the "small steps", it may be possible to tackle the big problems in the future. In this respect, the Davos Summit constitutes a radical change in the policies of Turkey and Greece.

If one disregards the tacit dropping of the unfruitful maximum positions by both sides, only Özal actually made a substantial advance performance: his announcement that the problem of the Greek minority would be solved in Istanbul.

The development of Davos until Özal's visit to Athens June 1988

And Özal kept his word. On 6 February, the Turkish Foreign Ministry announced the repeal of the 1964 secret decree that had put the property rights of the Greek minority in Turkey on hold. This affected about 12,000 Greeks who had left Turkey in 1964 in the wake of the first Cyprus crisis. The properties affected by that decree were estimated at around $300 million. Athens had announced in the summer of 1986 that it would not agree to the revival of the EC-Turkey Association Agreement until the decree was repealed. Now Athens welcomed the announcement, but wanted to wait for it to become concrete.

On 8 February, a cooperation agreement on road transport was signed in Ankara. The next day, the State Secretary in the Turkish Foreign Ministry, Nuzhet Kandemir, appeared in Athens. He delivered a personal message from Özal to Papandreou. After talks with Foreign Minister Papoulias, it was announced that the committees decided in Davos would be set up at the end of May. Both committees were to be chaired by the relevant ministers. A symptom of the new climate between the two countries can be seen in the fact that during this period the well-known Piri Reis was taking measurements of water pollution in the Aegean, even passing through Greek territorial waters, without any agitation from Athens. On 5 February, Papandreou informed the Cypriot foreign minister about the Davos talks. The assumption that Nicosia was disgruntled about the handling of the Cyprus problem and therefore only lakovou appeared in Athens instead of Kyprianou himself is probably unfounded in view of the fact that the election of the president was imminent in Cyprus. On 9 February, Papandreou informed the PASOK deputies of the content of the talks in Davos, and in Ankara, President Evren announced that his trip to Northern Cyprus had been postponed for the time being. In the following days, critical voices increased in Athens. In particular, it was criticised that Papandreou had been satisfied with Özal's statement that there were no missing persons. On 16 February, the Athens government spokesperson announced that the question of missing persons would be a topic of the renewed meeting of the two prime ministers within the framework of the NATO summit. On 18 February, the Athens Defence Ministry announced that the number of airspace violations had decreased considerably in the previous two weeks and that three manoeuvres planned for March had been cancelled. Obviously, Ankara was trying to live up to the "spirit of Davos". On 20 February, Archbishop Iakovos of North and South America reported that Özal had categorically assured him that the 12,000 Greeks who had left Istanbul in 1964 could return. He had even promised to reopen the Halki Theological Seminary.

Presidential elections were held in Cyprus on 21 February. The winner was the independent candidate Georgios Vassiliou. On the same day, Papandreou spoke at the Officers' Club in Loannina. On that occasion, he made an astonishing statement: *"For a long time, Cyprus and Greece have been talking about a triangle in which Greece urges the United States to urge Turkey to solve the problems. I think this process has now fallen behind. That is why we have to rely on our own capabilities. We can lay the foundations for peace with Turkey through dialogue at eye level."*[1]

On 25 February, Foreign Ministers Papoulias and Yilmaz met in Belgrade within the framework of the Balkan Conference to prepare for the meeting of the Premiers. It was announced that Ankara had also agreed to talks with Sofia. A day later, it became known that Özal had made a gesture to Athens Mayor Evert, who was visiting Istanbul and Ankara, on the issue of missing persons. He proposed to solve this problem within the framework of the UN by reactivating the competent committee.

On 3 and 4 March, the second meeting between Özal and Papandreou took place in Brussels in the framework of the NATO Summit. Again there was an extremely frank exchange of views. At the end of the meeting, a 1O-point communique was again published, which again contained some concrete measures to improve the climate between the two countries. The full text of the communiqué reads as follows:

1 The Prime Ministers of Greece and Turkey met in Brussels on 3rd -4th March 1988. Their discussions were conducted in a constructive spirit and in an atmos-phere of good will.

2 The two Prime Ministers decided upon ways to promote the rapprochement between the two countries in the light of the new positive momentum in their relations, following the Davos meeting.

3 In order to (acilitate this process the two Prime Minisers decided that the two countries abstain from any action or declaration which would undermine the spirit of Davos.

4 The two Prime Ministers decided that within March a subcommittee of the Political Committee, consisting of diplomats and military experts, be convened, under the supervision of the two Ministers of Foreign Affairs, in order to examine issues relating to the conduct of national military exercises as weil as to problems concerning the flights of military aircraft.

5 As regards the humanitarian question of missing persons in Cyprus, it was agreed to recommend to the parties concerned that the Committee on Missing Persons comprising representatives of the two communities on th island and an ICRC representative, as appointed by the Secretary General of the UN, should be reactivated. The Committee should be provided with every possible assistance so that it will be able to work in all possible ways to carry out its task. The Greek and the Turkish Prime Ministers also exchanged information on missing persons as supplied by the two communities on the island. Both parties stated that this issue should not constitute the subject of any form of political exploitation.

6 The Prime Minister of Turkey stated that, following the repeal of the Decree of 1964, the revenue from real estate property of Greek nationals in Turkey could be freely invested in Turkey. He also stated that in this context the Turkish government will take the necessary measures with a view to fully restoreing the rights of the Greek nationals in accordance with Turkish legislation.

---

1 *Athens News Agency,* 23 February 1988.
"For a long time, Greece and Cyprus have been talking about a triangular relationship, with Greece pressuring the United States to put pressure on Turkey to solve the problems. I believe that we have moved beyond that process. Therefore, we have to rely on our own capabilities. We can lay the foundations for peace with Turkey ourselves through dialogue on the basis of equality".

7 *In consideration of positive developments in this respect the Greek Prime Minister stated that the Greek side would give its consent so that the signing of the Adaptation Protocol to the Ankara Agreement of 1964 and the Additional Protocol thereto, following the accession of Greece to the European Communities.... becomes possible be fore the covening of the Association Council on 25th April 1988.*

8 *The two Prime Ministers also reviewed the political situation in the region. the results of the meeting of the Foreign Ministers of the Balkan countries, and the Iran-Iraq war.*

9 *The two Prime Ministers that the two committees will meet in Athens and Ankara respectively, on 26th May 1988. The Prime Minister of Turkey accepted an invitation extended by the Prime Minister of Greece to pay an official visit to Greece from 13th to 15th June 1988.*

10 *Finally the two Prime Ministers expreseedtheir satisfaction as regards the improvement of the climate between the two countries since their meeting in Davos.*

Both sides agreed to refrain from provocations of any kind that could undermine the "spirit of Davos" from now on. In order to prevent possible friction in the Aegean, a sub-committee of the political committee should be established to study the problems of military exercises and flights in the area. Papandreou accepted Ozal's proposal to reactivate the UN Committee on Missing Persons. In return for the lifting of that secret decree of 1964, Papandreou promised that Greece would sign that so-called adaptation agreement to the EC-Turkey Association Agreement. Finally, the dates were set for the first meeting of the two committees and Özal's visit to Athens.

The euphoria that had set in after the Brussels summit quickly evaporated in Athens. On 11 March, Papandreou had to face harsh criticism from the opposition in a debate on foreign policy. Opposition leader Mitsotakis accused the head of government of harming Greek interests through his "secret diplomacy". The Davos and Brussels meetings had been a fiasco. Papandreou had manoeuvred Greece into a position of weakness. Papandreou had abandoned his previously propagated "proud foreign policy", which had made the withdrawal of Turkish troops from Cyprus a condition for starting a dialogue with Ankara. Papandreou only gives the impression of a genuine peace policy, in fact he only has the 1989 elections in mind. In other words, the Greek opposition viewed the policy of rapprochement from a party-political point of view.

However, the climate of bilateral relations between Ankara and Athens in March 1988 remained friendly. On 29 March, Mikis Theodorakis, in his capacity as head of a delegation of the Greek-Turkish Friendship Committee, delivered a personal message from Papandreou to Özal. Özal expressed his opinion that his upcoming visit to Athens would be an important step forward. Although there was opposition to the Rapprochement in both countries, he was optimistic. On 30 March, Özal even appeared at a reception hosted by the Greek ambassador in Ankara to celebrate Greek independence, pointing out that it was in this very building that the treaty between Kemal Atatürk and Eleftherios Venizelos was signed in 1930.

On the same day, talks began in Athens of the sub-committee agreed in Brussels on military exercises in the Aegean. On 31 March, Theodorakis returned from Ankara and reported his positive impressions to Papandreou. Before that, however, Theodorakis had made some ill-considered statements in an interview, which were immediately exploited by the opposition for party political purposes. On 1 April, the work of the sub-committee ended. The final communiqué spoke of a good and serious atmosphere of the talks, but it became known that no substantial results had been achieved. Both sides had stated their positions and listened carefully to each other, which in itself was progress. On 3 April, Papandreou addressed Greek-Turkish relations in a speech in Larissa. In particular, he welcomed the fact that Ankara had passed a law retroactively repealing the 1964 secret decree. The next day he announced that PASOK would join the Greek-Turkish Friendship Committee.

In mid-April, the first tensions appeared again. On 13 April, State Secretary Irmgard Adam-Schwätzer came to Athens to clarify the question of EC financial aid to Turkey. Bonn was of the opinion that the planned funds of 600 million ECU should be released at the meeting of the EC Association Council on 25 April. Athens took the position that these funds should only be released after the withdrawal of Turkish troops from Cyprus and a change in Ankara's position on the human rights issue. Athens, however, was ready to join the Association Agreement.

On 15 April, it became known in Athens that Denktash had ordered the stamping of the passports of those entering through the UN checkpoint. It is unlikely that Denktash took this measure without the prior approval of certain Ankara circles, unless he was deliberately trying to thwart the Ankara-Athens détente. A conciliatory gesture followed on 17 April: Özal received the ecumenical patriarch in Istanbul for constructive talks. On 20 April, Greece signed, as agreed, the Agreement on Adaptation to the Turkish EC Association Agreement. At the same time, the Greek representative demanded that the Community adopt a common position on the withdrawal of Turkish troops from Cyprus and respect for human rights when negotiations with Turkey were to begin on 25 April. However, this proposal did not receive unanimous support.

Athens then tried to push through its position after all. One day later, Foreign Minister Papoulias stressed in Luxembourg that Ankara could only achieve something with the EC if the troops were withdrawn from Cyprus. Moreover, Athens would continue to block the ECU loan until the Turkish troops were withdrawn from Cyprus. The Luxembourg government agreed with him. Copenhagen signalled its support for the demand that human rights be respected.

On 22 April. State Secretary Theodoros Pangalos clarified the Greek position. The relations between the EC and Turkey were not part of the bilateral relations agreed in Davos. The "spirit of Davos" had no influence on the EC's relations with Turkey. If Bonn tries to avoid a reference to Cyprus in the opening statement, Athens will make its own statement. There would only be a common position if the other EC states adopted the Greek view. Athens obviously wanted to put pressure on its EC partners to adopt a clear position on the Cyprus question.

The Athens action gave ammunition to the hardliners in Ankara. Foreign Minister Yilmaz let it be known that the Turkish troops in Cyprus were not a subject for negotiation. Demanding a withdrawal of Turkish troops in order to normalise relations with the EC was like mixing apples with oranges. Then he spoke again of the "Turkish" minority in Thrace.

In Athens, this harsh reaction from Ankara was not expected and in order not to jeopardise what had been achieved so far, Papandreou sent the special envoy Christos Machairitsas to Ankara on 24 April with a message to Özal. Nevertheless, conflict broke out on the 25th. The foreign ministers of France, Spain, Portugal and Luxembourg supported the Greek demand, whereas the FRG tried hard to prevent a greater involvement of the EC in the Cyprus question. Secretary of State Pangalos, however, remained firm, and so the twelve Community foreign ministers finally accepted the Greek position. When Foreign Minister Yilmaz learned of this, he unapologetically cancelled the meeting of the Turkey-EC Association Council. Foreign Minister Yilmaz: "We will not be put under pressure!"[1] His colleague State Secretary for EC Affairs, Ali Bozer, had wanted to accept the Community's position.

There were different reactions in Ankara. Özal sent a very friendly message to Papandreou through Ambassador Machairitsas, stating that he was sticking to the planned visit to Athens. The Turkish Foreign Ministry protested against the presence of a Greek minister at an Armenian demonstration in Athens. Press reports spoke of differences within the Turkish leadership. Papandreou cleverly echoed this when he stated the following at a press conference in Oslo: When asked by a journalist for his opinion on Yilmaz's claim that the EC decision violated the spirit of Davos, Papandreou replied. "I haven't heard Mr Özal say anything to this effect."[2] The Turkish Foreign Ministry spokesman, on the other hand, said that Özal's visit to Athens was questionable. But on 28 April, Özal announced in an interview with Turkish Radio that he would definitely travel to Athens: The Davos and Brussels agreements did not imply any changes in behaviour with regard to existing problems. On 4 May, Özal told the BBC that nothing had changed in the climate of détente between Athens and Ankara. He blamed the collapse of negotiations with the EC on Foreign Minister Genscher, who had believed that Turkey would accept the Cyprus problem being put on the agenda. *"We could have accepted the discussion of this issue during the dinner,"* he added.[3]

On the same day, the Mayor of Istanbul, Bedreddin Dalan, visited Athens. When he laid a wreath at the Tomb of the Unknown Soldier in front of the parliament building, there were unpleasant clashes between Greek, Armenian, Kurdish, Turkish and Cypriot demonstrators with the police. Nevertheless, Dalan considered his visit a success that contributed to easing tensions. A few days later, Melina Merkouri visited Istanbul and Ankara, where she was warmly received and got the impression that Prime Minister Özal was seriously striving for friendship between the two countries. She registered with satisfaction Ankara's promise to support Greece's candidature for the 1996 Olympic Games.

These apparent improvements in the climate between the two countries, however, did not catch the attention of either the subordinate government agencies or the general public. On 18 May, the representatives of Greece and Turkey vetoed each other's plans at the NATO Planning Group meeting in Brussels, but this did not make headlines in Ankara or Athens. In Athens, the most diverse groups announced demonstrations for the visits of Yilmaz and Özal. And Papandreou informed the party leaders about the upcoming talks. Preparations entered the final round

On 19 May, Papandreou demanded that the Cyprus problem also be a topic of discussion between him and Özal. On 20 May, the European Parliament called on the EC foreign ministers to put pressure on Turkey so that Ankara would present a precise timetable for the withdrawal of its troops and settlers. Özal reacted immediately. In an interview with Hurriyet on 22 May, he declared his willingness to discuss Cyprus. However, only with Papandreou. The European Parliament's resolution was of little help, he said, as it only made things more complicated. Turkey and Greece play an important role in Cyprus. More important, however, were the two ethnic groups. They should get back into the conversation.

---

1 Gerd Höhler in *Frankfurter Rundschau,* 2 May1988.

2 *Athens News Agency,* 28. April 1988. "Ich habe Herrn Özal nichts in diese Richtung sagen hören " - "I have not heard Mr Özal say anything in this direction.

3 Athens News Agency, 5 Mayi 1988.
"Wir hätten eine Diskussion über dieses Thema während des Abendsessens akzeptieren können". - "We could have accepted a discussion on this issue during the dinner".

On 23 May, Yilmaz arrived with a large entourage for the first meeting of the Political Committee agreed in Davos. The visit started on a bad note: extremists attempted bomb attacks on vehicles belonging to Turkish diplomats. Nevertheless, Yilmaz was friendly in his first TV interview, but warned against too high hopes. On the same day, the talks of the Economic Committee also began in Ankara.

While demonstrators in the centre of Athens articulated their displeasure against Yilmaz's visit, the commission met in the hermetically sealed seaside resort of Vouliagmeni. Already at the first meeting, where the agenda was to be set, confrontation ensued. Yilmaz demanded that the talks should also deal with the Aegean problem and the Turkish minority in Thrace. When the Greek delegation refused, saying that Greece's sovereignty and territorial integrity could not be negotiated, it was finally agreed to leave out the thorny issues and turn to more solvable problems. The more sensitive issues were to be discussed by the two prime ministers.

Once agreement had been reached, two working groups were set up. The first working group dealt with "confidence-building measures". Its topics were manoeuvres, military flights and statements that could violate the spirit of Davos. Another topic was the lifting of the mutual veto in NATO. The second working group discussed practical issues such as abolishing the visa requirement for diplomats, improving the accommodation of diplomatic missions, combating smuggling and drug trafficking.

The talks ended on 26 May. The results were, as could be expected, not overwhelming, but they included a number of confidence-building measures. The ministers signed a memorandum on military activities in the Aegean, in which they assured each other that they would respect the sovereignty and territorial integrity of their countries as well as the right to free use of the international waters and air zones of the Aegean Sea and refrain from anything that could lead to tensions. In concrete terms, this meant: Any kind of military exercise should henceforth be announced to the other side through diplomatic channels. In addition, both sides undertook to refrain from manoeuvres that would result in a prolonged closure of sea areas. During the high tourist season and on religious and national holidays, manoeuvres were to be dispensed with altogether.

It was also agreed to abandon the previous practice of mutual blocking within NATO. Diplomats should no longer be subject to visa requirements. Both sides would refrain from making provocative statements and would influence their countries' media accordingly. Finally, it was agreed to cooperate in the fight against smuggling, drug trafficking and terrorism.

The results of the negotiations of the Economic Committee in Ankara were of course far more productive. Close cooperation in a wide range of sectors was agreed upon and a number of concrete measures were envisaged. Finally, closer cultural cooperation was agreed upon.

In addition to these official negotiations, Yilmaz also found time to discuss Greek-Turkish relations with opposition leader Mitsotakis. According to informed sources, Yilmaz informed Mitsotakis that he would soon visit Northern Cyprus in order to convince Denktash of the necessity of resuming the inter-communal talks. If Denktash did not respond, Özal would take matters into his own hands. It can be assumed that Yilmaz also informed Papandreou of this at their meeting on 26 May. The accuracy of this information is supported both by Vassiliou's calm reaction when he was approached by journalists a few days later about Yilmaz's forthcoming visit to the North,[1] and by the restrained reaction of the Athens government during Yilmaz's visit on 22 June.

The days leading up to Özal's visit were quite hectic for Athens. On 28 May, Vassiliou interrupted his flight to the UN General Assembly for a few hours in Athens to be informed about the results of the negotiations. At the same time, Vassiliou presented his plans. On the occasion of Vasos Lyssaridis' visit to Athens on 31 May, Papandreou stated that Cyprus would always be a national priority. On 3 June, in New York, where he visited the UN, Papoulias demanded that Ankara make a gesture of goodwill. He expected Ankara to announce before Özal's visit that part of the Turkish troops would be withdrawn from Cyprus. On 5 June, a three-day parliamentary debate began in Athens, during which opposition leader Mitsotakis called for condemnation of the government's domestic and foreign policies. One day later, Özal commented on the Athenian demands: as long as pressure is exerted, he cannot do anything. In addition, the elections in Greece were approaching. But the fundamental problems could only be tackled by a government with a new mandate. As soon as there is an agreement on Cyprus, Ankara will reduce its troops. Özal had originally even planned to withdraw some troops as a sign of goodwill.

On 8 June, Kyprianou visited Athens. After a discussion with Papandreou, he told the press that he and the Greek Prime Minister shared the opinion that the policy pursued during his term in office had been successful. It had succeeded in drawing the attention of world opinion to the Cyprus problem and its three basic problems. He mentioned the withdrawal of Turkish troops and settlers, the question of human rights and the problem of guarantees. Unlike Papandreou, however, he did not believe in a change in Turkish policy, neither Ankara's nor Denktash's.

On 10 June, Foreign Ministers Yilmaz and Shultz met at the NATO Spring Meeting in Madrid. Shultz expressed his hope that the Papandreou-Oezal meeting would be a success. success. In addition, the efforts of the UN Secretary General to find a solution to the Cyprus conflict were to be supported. Meanwhile, opposition to Özal's visit was growing in Athens. There was practically no political group that did not in some way express reservations about Özal's visit. Even the PASOK weekly Exormisis; found militant tones when it stated: If necessary, one would return to the pre-Davos policy, but then in a better position. Greece had taken the initiative in the developments leading to Davos and paved the way for a real reconciliation. Now it is up to Turkey to prove that it really wants peace. If developments stalled, Turkey would have to explain to the world why it was pursuing such an intransigent line. This was followed by a list of Greek essentials and the indication that Papandreou regarded Özal's visit as a working visit.

It was clear that this article had not appeared without the knowledge or against the will of the PASOK party leader. Clearly, a catch-all position was being built here in case the talks with Özal failed.

---

1 *Athens News Agency*, 7 June 1988.

Özal's historic visit to Athens

Özal arrived in Athens at noon on 13 June. This was the first visit of a Turkish prime minister to Athens in 36 years. In view of the opposition, extreme security measures had been taken. The talks lasted until 15 June.

The joint final communiqué spoke of the "constructive spirit", the atmosphere of "goodwill" and "mutual understanding". The two premiers welcomed the results of the political and economic committees. They agreed that the process of détente requires patience, mutual respect, goodwill and determination. Finally, it was announced that the committees would continue their work at the beginning of September. Papandreou would visit Turkey in the autumn. At first sight, these were more than meagre results of such a summit meeting, since they only set down what had already been achieved so far.

However, from the positive reactions of Mitsotakis, who after his meeting with Özal spoke of a new phase in the Greek-Turkish dialogue, it can be concluded that the talks have made substantial progress. Papandreou gave a similar impression when he spoke of light at the end of the tunnel. Papandreou stressed that the Greek-Turkish rapprochement depended on progress in the Cyprus issue. Özal, too, was quite positive at his press conference shortly before his return flight. He noted that the Cyprus problem was an international one, but still affected bilateral relations. It had to be solved primarily through talks between the ethnic groups. He hoped that the recent meeting between Vassiliou and Denktash, mediated by de Cuellar, would produce results. As soon as an agreement was reached, the Turkish troops would be withdrawn. Then Özal became visionary. EC accession for both Turkey and Cyprus would solve all problems. Back in Ankara, the Athens News Agency correspondent asked Özal if Papandreou's visit to Ankara would be richer in results. özal replied: *"Of course it will be. Just as my future visit will be. even richer (in results)".*[1]

Although the outcome of the Athens summit was not very impressive at first glance, one thing became very clear once again: both sides want to continue the process of rapprochement. Progress on less prestigious issues is easily possible. And paradoxical as it may sound, of the two major problem areas - the Aegean conflict and the Cyprus conflict - the latter is easier to resolve. This brings the analysis back to the Cyprus question.

The Cyprus problem from January until the resumption of intercommunal talks in August 1988

On 14 February 1988, the first round of the Cypriot presidential elections took place, in which none of the candidates achieved the required absolute majority. The independent candidate Georgios Vassiliou emerged victorious from the second round on 21 February with 51.63 per cent of the vote. His fiercest rival, the conservative Glafkos Kliridis, was only narrowly defeated with 48.37 percent. The election of Vassiliou can probably be interpreted as a rejection by the majority of voters of the previous Cyprus policy and as a generational change.

After his election, Vassiliou declared that he would seek rapprochement and sincere cooperation with the Turkish Cypriots. He also declared his willingness to meet with Denktash, but without preconditions; that is, he rejected Denktash's demand for a "meeting between presidents". On the occasion of his swearing-in on 28 February, he proposed a meeting between him and Özal. Then he presented his conception for the solution of the Cyprus problem: Withdrawal of Turkish troops and settlers, respect for the rights of citizens to move freely, settle

1 *Athens News Agency*, 16 June 1988. "Of course. Just as my future visit will also be richer [in results]" .

freely and own property. Refugees should be allowed to return. International guarantees should exclude any unilateral intervention. Talks were useful, but they should not be held for their own sake. To resolve the international implications, he said, it was necessary to convene an international conference within the UN framework. He would reactivate the National Council, in which all parties are represented, in order to put the policy of solving the Cyprus problem on a broader basis. This Council should develop a comprehensive solution plan. If a solution is found, it will be presented to the people in a referendum. Until a solution is found, however, the island's defence capability must be increased. At the same time, he would launch a diplomatic offensive to remind the world of the Cyprus problem. Domestically', he would strive to restore confidence between Greek and Turkish Cypriots. In foreign policy, he will steer a course of non-alignment.[1]

The Foreign Ministry in Ankara rejected the request to talk to Özal. The right contact person, it said, was Denktash. The Foreign Minister of the North, Kenan Atakol, accused Vassiliou of pursuing the same intransigent policy as his predecessor. Opposition leader Özgur urged restraint and Ismet Kotak said in Kibris Postasi that Vassiliou should be given time; the world would certainly recognise who was intransigent. Özal's Detente course was obviously causing headaches for the leadership of the North. On 12 March, Denktash proposed the conclusion of a non-aggression pact between the north and south of Cyprus, the aim of which would clearly be the upgrading of the north. At the same time, however, the government of the north prohibited journalists and artists from participating in an exhibition in the south. In mid--March, Vassiliou visited Athens to coordinate his policy with that of Athens. Apparently, there was a broad convergence of views. In the meantime, Denktash began to fear any marital agreements between Özal and Papandreou over Cyprus. He therefore told the Miliyet newspaper on 13 March that Turkey had no right to make concessions concerning the Turkish Cypriots. Özgür then accused Denktash of trying to threaten Ankara and poison the positive climate of Davos. On 16 March, Denktash repeated his statement: no one could impose an agreement on Northern Cyprus. Denktash's fears were also shared by Ismet Kotak, who expressed suspicion that secret agreements had been made at the Brussels meeting between Papandreou and Özal. Denktash's outburst prompted Ankara to intervene. Özal's foreign policy advisor, Cem Duna and a senior official of the Turkish Foreign Ministry appeared in Northern Cyprus on a secret mission and tried to calm Denktash down. However, Denktash could not be convinced that there had been no change in Ankara's foreign policy. On 21 March, he told Milliyet that no solution would be imposed from outside.

On 24 March, Denktash flew to London for a seminar on the Cyprus question. At Izmir airport, he told the newspaper Tercüman that he had made a mistake in his interpretation of Davos. At the same time, he offered Vassiliou talks without preconditions that could take place during Vassiliou's stay in London. Vassiliou rejected the proposal: such a meeting would have to be carefully prepared if it was to produce results.

Denktash then accused Vassiliou of the same intransigence as his predecessors in office. The Greek Cypriots rejected the recognition of the North as a state. This was irrelevant; the state existed. If they were serious about the reunification of Cyprus, the way would be through the recognition of the "Turkish Republic of Northern Cyprus". The two states would then ne-

1 *Athens News Agency*, 29 February 1988.

gotiate whether they should unite or not. If the Greek side did not accept this, the efforts to recognise the northern state would continue. Shortly afterwards, Denktash specified his ideas: They would wait for the meeting between Özal and Papandreou in June. If Vassiliou had not returned to the conference table by then, they would work for recognition. Özgür criticised Denktash's attitude. On the one hand, he stressed at every opportunity that he accepted the UN proposal of 29 March 1986, but on the other hand, he had now made a complete course correction. After his return from London, Denktash went one step further. He stated that even in a reunited Cyprus there would be no "'settlers" from the south in the north.

At the end of March, Vassiliou visited London to secure the support of Margaret Thatcher, who would visit Ankara on 6 April. He asked Mrs. Thatcher to support his proposal of a meeting with Özal in Ankara. He said he was prepared to meet with Denktash within the framework of the UN, but he could only talk about the withdrawal of Turkish troops and settlers with Özal, who was responsible for this. The British Prime Minister assured that Great Britain would never recognise the "Turkish Republic of Northern Cyprus" as a state. Afterwards, Vassiliou had a detailed discussion on the Cyprus problem with the State Department's coordinator for the Cyprus question, James Wilkinson, in London. The latter then flew to Ankara, where Foreign Minister Yilmaz, however, refused to talk to him because Wilkinson allegedly wanted to plead for flexibility and concessions on the Cyprus issue. The newspaper Milliyet reported that the Turkish government refused to bow to American pressure.

The Turkish government was more conciliatory towards Margaret Thatcher. In the joint final press conference on 8 April, Mrs. Thatcher stated that the election of Vassiliou and the recent improvements in Greek-Turkish relations had created a new situation. Progress could be made on the Cyprus issue. It was necessary to initiate negotiations between the leaders of the two communities under the auspices of Perez de Cuellar. Özal agreed.

On 9 April, Denktash presented his ideas to the newspaper Birlik: There are two states in Cyprus. If these states were to be united, this could only happen on the condition that the independence of each one was preserved. An unrestricted right to freedom of movement was out of the question. A central government could only have as much power as the individual states granted it. Denktash's ideas of a reunited Cyprus were clearly moving towards a loose confederation.

On 12 April, the newspaper Günes published an article according to which Özal was allegedly working on a plan to withdraw some troops from Cyprus in order to make a gesture to world opinion and to promote Greek-Turkish rapprochement. In return, Athens should persuade Vassiliou to meet with Denktash. This would be a first step towards solving the Cyprus problem. Allegedly, Özal and Papandreou had agreed on this via the "hot wire" between Athens and Ankara. The Turkish Foreign Ministry, however, views this activity with suspicion.

Meanwhile, in Cyprus, the long-time General Secretary of AKEL, Ezekias Papaioannou, had died on 10 April and the Cypriot government had ordered a state funeral for 14 April. When Özker Özgür, accompanied by some of his party's functionaries and some journalists, wanted to cross the demarcation line to the south on that day, the Turkish border police refused. The "foreign ministry" of the north announced that crossing the border was only allowed with passports that had to be stamped. Özgür protested against this arbitrary measure, saying it was contrary to the "spirit of Davos" and only escalated the politics of hostility. Nicosia reacted by stating that anyone going from the south to the north and having their passport stamped would not be allowed to return to the south. At the same time, the Cypriot government lodged a protest with the UN. Thus the situation in Cyprus was again as confused as it had hardly been before.

The Foreign Ministry in Ankara took the position that Denktash's action was the decision of the sovereign "Turkish Republic of Northern Cyprus". Washington did not accept this and intervened. tn Ankara, Washington and New York, US diplomats indicated that Ankara should put pressure on Denktash to withdraw his measure. On 22 April, Denktash announced that he was ready to talk to Vassiliou about the border issue, provided it was on "equal terms". A day later, the newspaper Günes reported that Özal had wanted to withdraw some troops from Cyprus before his visit to Athens as a gesture of goodwill, but that the Turkish general staff had taken this idea very coldly. Meanwhile, it became known that the border police in the north had refused entry to three EC representatives when they refused to have their passports stamped.

Obviously, however, the superpowers were not prepared to let the climate of detente be disturbed by these quarrels and took action.

On 28 April, the Soviet Special Envoy, Igor Andropov, visited Nicosia. At a press conference he welcomed Vassilous' course and announced that the Cyprus problem was on the agenda of the Reagan-Gorbatchov summit at the end of May. At the same time, it was announced that Vassilous would be making a state visit to the Soviet Union in the foreseeable future. This prompted Denktash to make the following statement on 6 May: Should Moscow receive Vassiliou as the president of the whole of Cyprus and also talk to him about the north, this would constitute an unfriendly act against the Turkish Cypriot people:[1]

At the same time, the first Deputy Foreign Minister of the Soviet Union, Vorontsov, appeared in Ankara, where he also raised the Cyprus problem.

Meanwhile, the Americans increased their pressure on Ankara. The US ambassador in Ankara visited Foreign Minister Yilmaz and expressed US concern about the developments in Cyprus. Denktash's action, he said, violated the Davos spiri . At the same time, the State Department asked the Turkish ambassador in Washington to put pressure on Denktash to lift the "passport measures". Although Foreign Minister Yilmaz refused to put pressure on Denktash, he postponed his planned May trip to Northern Cyprus until after Özal's visit to Athens.

On 5 May, Yilmaz and lakovou met at a dinner hosted by Luxembourg's Foreign Minister , Jacques Poos, in Strasbourg in honour of the Council of Europe Foreign Ministers gathered there. A lively exchange of views soon developed between the two foreign ministers across the table. It became clear - according to press reports - that Ankara urgently needed a solution to the Cyprus problem, but did not want to be forced to find a solution at the expense of the Turkish Cypriots. Turkey had accepted that Cyprus would be a point of discussion between Özal and Papandreou. The "spirit of Davos" also extended to the Cyprus problem.[2]

On 10 May, Hurriyet published an interview with Vassiliou in which he made his position clear: he wanted to talk to Özal in order to discuss the international aspects of the Cyprus problem, such as the withdrawal of troops and the issue of settlers. With Denktash he wanted to discuss internal Cypriot issues such as the future constitution. Guarantees, he said, were unnecessary. However, if guarantees were deemed necessary, they should have an international character and protect all Cypriots equally. No one should be given the right to intervene in Cyprus ever again. He was in favour of the earliest possible start of substantive negotiations.

---

1 Denktash on the Northern Cyprus Radio on 6 May 1988.

2 *Athens News Agency*, 9 May 1988.

He welcomed the fact that the Cyprus problem was being discussed at the Reagan-Gorbachev summit, because problems discussed at such summits were getting closer to a solution. He said he supported the UN's efforts and therefore refused to put forward any proposals himself which were only for self-promotion but did not help the cause. It was clear that a withdrawal of troops in one fell swoop was impossible, but he expected a statement from Turkey that it was ready to withdraw its troops according to a fixed timetable once a reasonable solution had been found. A solution to the Cyprus problem would also be of political and economic benefit to Turkey.

In mid-May, efforts to bring movement to the Cyprus issue intensified. On 20 May, the European Parliament passed a resolution calling for the reunification of the island and the withdrawal of Turkish troops.[1] On the same day, the senior UN official, Gustav Feissel, made a surprise visit to Cyprus to present new proposals from de Cuellar to both sides on the resumption of ethnic talks. A first meeting between Vassiliou and Denktash should take place as soon as possible in a European capital. Vassiliou immediately accepted de Cuellar's proposals and informed the National Council. Feissel then went to the north to sound out Denktash's willingness to meet. Denktash accepted "in principle". On the 21st, the EC Commissioner for Mediterranean Affairs, Claude Cheysson, appeared in Nicosia. He stressed that the division of Cyprus was unacceptable and demanded the withdrawal of Turkish troops. In the USA, Republican Senator Larry Pressier told Congress that now was the right time for a solution to the Cyprus problem. The US government should contribute to the solution. President Reagan reacted promptly and called for the opening of negotiations between the Cypriot communities on 26 May.

On 31 May, de Cuellar and Vassiliou had a first discussion on the mode of the first round of talks. On 2 June, Vassiliou addressed the UN General Assembly. He made a rather interesting proposal: if Turkey withdrew its troops and settlers from Cyprus, the Cypriot government would disband the National Guard. The money thus saved would be paid into a fund to be used for the promotion of the economically backward (Turkish-Cypriot) areas. Security was to be provided by an international UN peacekeeping force. On 5 June, Vassiliou met with Wilkinson, who presented him with an invitation from Reagan for an official visit. In the following days, further talks took place between Vassiliou and the foreign ministers of Britain (Howe), the FRG and Spain (Ordonez), all of whom assured him of their support. After Vassiliou's departure, Özal appeared in New York. According to press reports, he timed his arrival so that a "chance" meeting with Vassiliou was out of the question. In conversation with de Cuellar, it was determined that a meeting between Vassiliou and Denktash would take place without preconditions. Afterwards Özal went to Houston for medical treatment.

After Vassiliious and özal's departure, de Cuellar presented his six-month report on UNFICYP activities to the Security Council. He welcomed the latest developments. In particular, he said, the distrust between the ethnic groups on Cyprus must be reduced. This was primarily their task, but others could contribute. If Ankara reduced the number of its troops in the north, this would be very helpful. He appealed to the Turkish government to take this step. He had made precise proposals to the two ethnic group leaders on the basis of the 1977 and 1979 Agreements for the opening of negotiations.

In Ankara, this development was obviously observed with concern. Articles appeared in the Turkish press talking about differences between Özal and Denktash on the one hand and

1 Text of the resolution in: *Zypern Bulletin,* 12:11 (1 June 1988). pp. 2-3.

friction between the Turkish prime minister and the foreign ministry on the other. It cannot be ruled out that the hardliners wanted to use Özal's absence to create a few internal Turkish "falts accomplis" before Özal's meeting with Papandreou. Probably for this reason, the "foreign minister" of the North, Atakol, was invited to Ankara for talks with Yilmaz and President Evren. Evren took the opportunity to state on television after his meeting with Atakol that there would be no withdrawal of troops from Cyprus, clearly exceeding his constitutional powers and preventing Özal from making a gesture in Athens on this issue. In the press conference at the end of Atakol's visit, Foreign Minister Yilmaz admitted that there had been differences of opinion, but that they had now been resolved. American diplomatic circles spoke of a "direct dialogue" between the Turkish army and the "Turkish Republic of Northern Cyprus" , in which firm guarantees had been given to Atakol.[1]

On 9 June, Yilmaz and US Secretary of State Shultz had a lengthy discussion on Greek--Turkish relations on the sidelines of the NATO' Spring Meeting in Madrid. Shultz welcomed Özal's upcoming visit to Athens. On Cyprus, he said, the US was fully behind de Cuellar's initiative. "It's a shame that the initiative has not progressed. We hope that the leaders of the two communities in Cyprus will find a way to promote this initiative". President Evren is expected in Washington shortly, "which will give us the opportunity to discuss these matters again".[2]

After returning from Madrid on 11 June, Yilmaz accused the UN Secretary General of exceeding his authority with his last report calling for a partial withdrawal of Turkish troops. The troops would remain in Cyprus as long as Turkey considered it necessary. In the following days, Özal's visit to Athens took place, which has already been described.

On 16 June, it was announced in Nicosia that there would be a meeting between Denktash and Vassiliou. On the same day, an article appeared in the Turkish newspaper Sabah accusing Denktash of slowly becoming a mortgage for Turkish foreign policy. He had apparently taken such a liking to his "presidency" that he was not inclined to give it up. On 20 June, Özgür attacked Denktash: He said that the only one who did not want a solution to the conflict was Denktash, but Washington, London and Ankara wanted a solution. Denktash countered the next day on Northern Radio: before a solution to the Cyprus problem, the "Turkish Republic of Northern Cyprus" had to be recognised. The existence of the "TRNC" was a fact and his delegation would participate in the forthcoming negotiations as official representatives of the "TRNC", whether it suited the Greek Cypriots or not. Denktash was obviously trying to stonewall.

On 22 June, Yilmaz arrived in the North for an "official" visit. While subsequent press statements again referred to the "complete harmony" of views, at the same time Yilmaz signalled that Turkey no longer insisted that the 29 March (1986) Agreement must be the basis for negotiations. Turkey, he said, was in favour of a federal solution to the Cyprus problem. In view of the extremely positive reaction of the opposition (Özgür spoke of complete agreement), it may be concluded that Denktash absolutely did not agree with Yilmaz's views. The general secretary of Denktash's party (NUP) was of the opinion that maintaining the status quo

---

1 *Cumhuriyetam* 8 June 1988.

2 *Athens News Agency*. 11 June 1988.
"It is a shame that the initiative has not made any progress. We hope that the leaders of the two communities in Cyprus will find a way to promote the initiative". President Evren is expected in Washington shortly, "which will give us a chance to discuss these issues again".

was the best solution. The settlers' party also reacted very cautiously to Yilmaz's proposals. In view of this situation, Yilmaz seems to have asked Denktash to come to Ankara for talks. Therefore, at the end of the Turkish Foreign Minister's visit, it was announced that Denktash would meet with Evren before negotiations began.

On 26 June, President Evren flew to the USA for talks with de Cuellar, representatives of the US Congress and the administration. US Secretary of State Shultz gave Evren to understand that the meeting between Vassiliou and Denktash had to take place. Evren was flexible in suggesting that Ankara no longer insisted on the 29 March agreement. The State Department was satisfied. After Evren's return to Turkey, Denktash was summoned to Ankara. From the manner of the reception -neither Evren nor Özal appeared to greet the "President of the Turkish Republic of Northern Cyprus" at the airport.[1] it was clear that Denktash had been ordered to report. After discussions with Evren, Özal and Yilmaz, it was announced that Denktash was ready to resume intercommunal talks without preconditions.

In the following days, Denktash repeatedly tried to delay the start of talks, but de Cuellar's representative on the ground, Camillion, did not let up. In a kind of "shuttle diplomacy" he cleared resistance out of the way. At the same time, international pressure intensified. On 12 July, when Evren visited London, Mrs. Thatcher told Evren that she wanted talks to begin. Queen Elizabeth made a similar statement. At the same time, all the national newspapers in Britain published an appeal by 73 leading figures in the country calling on Evren to contribute to the solution of the Cyprus problem.

On 21 July, Washington issued a similar appeal. On 25 July, the UN announced that the meeting would take place on 24 August. On 28 July, Vassiliou gave an interview to the Athens News Agency before leaving for the USA. Among other things, he stated: . not. at present, he said, there was a kind of "peace epidemic". Conflicts are being resolved everywhere. If Cyprus were to be excluded from this, it would be strangely. The solution of the Cyprus problem would depend mainly on Ankara. The US government obviously had an interest in the solution. It could make a substantial contribution by convincing Turkey to withdraw its occupation forces and to respect human rights. On 29 August, Vassiliou had a first meeting with Secretary of State Shultz. On 1 August he met with Reagan. Both agreed that no foreign troops should be stationed in any country and that human rights should be respected. Reagan, as well as Vice-President Bush afterwards, assured that they supported UN chief de Cuellar's initiative.

In the following days, Vassiliou informed other US administration figures of his intentions. At the same time, he tried to win broader support. On 3 August, he addressed the Center for Strategy and International Studies in Washington. He noted that US policy on Cyprus since 1974 had been characterised by inactivity, as the US considered Turkey to be of significant strategic importance. The US had therefore not put pressure on Turkey to moderate its policy towards Cyprus, with Washington ultimately favouring Ankara's policy. But now there is flexibility, a new policy.[2] On another occasion, Vassiliou said that he could agree to a gradual withdrawal of Turkish troops, but that this would have to be completed before the establishment of an all-Cypriot interim government. At the end of his trip, Vassiliou was extremely satisfied with its results.

---

1 The Ortam newspaper of 5 July 1988 spoke of Denktash being treated like a provincial mukhtar (village headman).

2 *Athens News Agency,* 4 August 1988.

On 4 August, US Secretary of Defence Carlucci visited Ankara on his return flight from Moscow. He met with Prime Minister Özat and President Evren to inform them of his talks with the Soviet government. Although Cyprus was not mentioned in the final communique, it may be assumed that Carlucci also addressed this problem.

Cyprus also began to prepare for the talks. On 29 July, the North lifted the passport regulations for foreigners and Maronites. Denktash withdrew to the mainland to prepare for the meeting. Özgür welcomed the upcoming negotiations, but had doubts about whether Denktash was serious. To emphasise his desire for a solution to the Cyprus problem, he started collecting signatures for a federal solution. On 9 August, it was announced that the meeting would take place in Geneva on 24 August. On 10 August, Vassiliou informed the National Council about the results of his trip to the USA. At the same time, it became known that the US Congress had passed a joint resolution expressing the hope that the upcoming meeting would be successful. Two days later, the National Council met again, and a negotiating strategy approved by all party leaders was set. .

Probably in order to make his views known in the north of the island, Vassiliou agreed to receive a group of Turkish Cypriot journalists in Nicosia for a talk. However, the authorities in the north did not allow the journalists from the opposition newspapers Yeniduzen, Ortam and Demokrat to leave. In the conversation itself, Vassiliou expressed little that was new. He had no patent solution for a federation. The starting point for all considerations would have to be the agreements of 1977 and 1979. Further details would have to be developed in the discussion. However, there must be a basic consensus, namely that Cyprus is one country. It is necessary to look for ways that lead towards each other and not away from each other. He understood the Turkish Cypriot side's need for security, the Greek side felt similarly, but security could be guaranteed without the presence of troops. He hoped that his first meeting with Denktash would develop into a good relationship. If there was enough goodwill, the Cyprus problem could be solved even before the June 1989 deadline for a solution.

In the following days, Denktash also spoke up again. although he repeatedly emphasised that he was in favour of a federal solution, interspersed with this were remarks that clearly showed that the whole direction did not suit him.

On 22 August, Vassiliou and Denktash arrived in Geneva. Both assured in press conferences that they were full of goodwill. On 23 August, Vassiliou first conferred with the members of the National Council accompanying him (Kliridis, Kyprianou, Lyssaridis and Christofias) to document the will of all Greek Cypriot parties for a solution. Afterwards, he gave an interview to Turkish television: He said it was important to forget the past and look forward. He could imagine a Cyprus in which Cypriots, Greeks and Turks alike, lived freely, felt safe and had the feeling of being equal citizens. Dialogue between the communities should begin as soon as possible. He hoped that the talks with Denktash would get off to a good start and that the actual negotiations would be conducted in a business-like manner. The next step would be the gradual withdrawal of Turkish troops. In order to restore the lack of trust between the ethnic groups, it was necessary to allow freedom of movement as soon as possible. The Turkish fears of Greek enosis efforts were groundless. The Greek side is in favour of the independence of Cyprus

Vassiliou then met with UN Secretary-General de Cuellar for final talks. In the afternoon, the same discussion took place between de Cuellar and Denktash. On 24 August, the decisive meeting took place at a working lunch organised by de Cueilar. Also present were de Cuellar's representative Goulding and the UN representative in Cyprus Oscar Camillion. In a neighbouring room, senior UN official Feissel gave Vassiliou and Denktash's advisors a meal.

At the end of the two-hour working lunch, de Cuellar went to a press conference with Vassiliou on his right and Denktash on his left. The ethnic leaders shook hands and smiled in front of the television cameras. Oe Cuellar announced that Vassiliou and Denktash would meet on 16 September at the Ledra Palace Hotel in the UN buffer zone between southern and northern Nicosia. This meeting would have a ceremonial character. The actual negotiations would start one day later. The two Cypriot leaders had agreed to meet without preconditions and to try to find a negotiated solution to the Cyprus problem by 1 June 1989. The working lunch gave both leaders the opportunity to get to know each other and to exchange views on the Cyprus problem. Both sides had accepted the 1977 and 1979 Agreements and the 1980, 1981 and 1984 UN documents as a basis for work, as well as the good offices of the UN Secretary-General.

Another meeting took place on the evening of the 24th. Before the conversation, Denktash stated that he was satisfied with the first meeting. He told Turkish television that there was nothing negative about Vassiliou. He had a good and open character. He was a person with whom one could talk seriously. The next day, before his flight back to Cyprus, Vassiliou stated that the meeting with de Cuellar and Denktash had exceeded his expectations. De Cuellar also expressed a similar sentiment and at the same time announced that both sides had agreed to meet with him in New York in October or early November to brief him on the state of negotiations reached by then.

The Developments after August 1988

The development of the overall complex of Greek-Turkish relations after Özal's visit to Athens is essentially shaped by Greek domestic political developments.

In his speech on 27 June 1988 at the EC summit in Hanover, Papandreou said that it was the task of the EC to deepen the process of European unification. For the immediate future, discussions and measures aimed at further expansion of the Community should be refrained from. In other words, this meant: Papandreou even rejected talks with Turkey on possible EC accession. On 1 July, Greece took over the EC presidency.

On 7 July, Foreign Minister Papoulias informed the EC Parliament in Strasbourg about the plans of the Greek government during its EC Presidency. Commenting on the Cyprus problem, he said that Cyprus is a member of the European family. The Cyprus issue affects the Community's relations with Ankara. The EC had expressed its interest in a solution and Greece would promote a solution based on unity, independence and territorial integrity during its presidency. Turkey could only expect something from the Community if it withdrew its troops from Cyprus.[1] On 10 July, Papoulias made a similar statement to the European Parliament's Political Affairs Committee.[2]

Özal was not put off by these statements. On the same day, he told the newspaper Milliyet that the dialogue with Papandreou would continue. He said that it was not a dialogue of the hard of hearing, but that they were listening to each other attentively. "We do not impose the condition of an immediate solution to all problems. We have not made any promises in this regard, neither from one side nor from the other ... we set out to correct relations between the two countries, and they are much better now than before ... a few years ago, one could have imagined such a rapprochement.[3]

1 *Athens News Agency,* 6 July 1988.
2 *Athens News Agency,* 11 July 1988.
3 ibidem.
"We are in no way making a condition that all problems will be solved immediately. Neither side has made any

On 25 July, Papandreou announced that he would not visit Ankara during Greece's EC presidency. However, the meeting of foreign ministers scheduled for September in Ankara would remain. As Papandreou did not give any further reasons in public, this announcement was met with incomprehension in the Turkish press. The actual reason for this announcement was Papandreou's unstable state of health, which was kept quiet for the time being for domestic political reasons. Özal, however, said that the process initiated in Davos was continuing.[1]

One day later, it became clear in Brussels that the EC was serious in its demand towards Turkey. The Budget Council of Ministers cancelled the EC credits of the 4th EC Financial Protocol for Turkey. The Greek government had refused to sign the 4th Financial Protocol because of human rights violations in Turkey and the continuing occupation of Cyprus. Until then, the EC Finance Ministers had always included the loans in the EC budget, but the European Parliament had always cancelled them.[2]

On 19 August, Foreign Minister Yilmaz reacted to Greek behaviour in the EC in an interview. *"Turkey has been amazed over certain 'unfortunate' statements, Greece's unfriendly attitude towards Turkey within the EEC, and certain approaches in the Aegean."* They will have to talk about this in September.[3] As the date for the first meeting between Vassiliou and Denktash was approaching, and probably also because Papandreou knew that he would soon be going to London for medical treatment, he sent his special envoy, Christos Machairitsas, with a personal message to Özal in Ankara on 21 August. Özal, while assuring that he shared Papandreou's view that the Davos process must continue, brought further progress in bilateral relations inlusse the link with the Greek elections.

On 23 August, as has already been shown, Vassiliou and Denktash met with Perez de Cuellar to open the new round of intercommunal talks in Geneva. Two days later Papandreou flew to London for medical treatment. The Papandreou-Vassiliou meeting planned after the Geneva talks had to be cancelled. On 30 August, Foreign Minister Papoulias made an official visit to Nicosia in order to be informed about the results of the Geneva talks. At the subsequent press conference, Papoulias showed subdued optimism about the upcoming intercommunal talks. However, if they fail, this would also have a negative effect on bilateral relations between Greece and Turkey. If Turkey really wanted to prove its goodwill, it could do so now by withdrawing its occupation forces from Cyprus. He agreed with the Cypriot leadership that the issue of the settlers, effective international guarantees and respect for the three freedoms had to be part of the solution. However, he foresaw difficulties with Denktash, who would certainly adopt an intransigent attitude. The Cypriot government's wish to start talks on full EC membership had been discussed and Greece would support such an application, but this was a delicate issue.[4]

On 5 September, the next round of talks between Ankara and Athens began. The political committee met in Ankara under the chairmanship of the two foreign ministers, Yilmaz and Papoulias. The economic committee met in Athens. In an interview with the English-language Turkish newspaper Daily News published on the day the conference began, Yilmaz had complained that Greece was putting artificial obstacles in the way of the rapprochement process.

promises in this direction ... We have started to improve relations between the two countries, and they are now much better than before ... A few years ago, no one could have imagined such a rapprochement".

1 *Athens News Agency,* 2 August 1988.

2 *Athens News Agency*, 2. July 1988.

3 *Athens News Agency*, 24 August 1988.

4 *Athens News Agency,* 31 August 1988.

"The fact that Greece is attempting to link the Cyprus problem with the process started at Davos is an example ... Greece was now maintaining that some of the issues which it initially agreed to discuss touch upon national sovereignty and cannot be negotiated." Despite this criticism, Yilmaz announced that they would discuss the problems at hand and try to find "grassroots solutions". In addition, it is important to create a climate of trust that will be helpful in solving the problems.[1]

Following the meeting of the political committee, Papoulias had a long discussion with Prime Minister Özal and President Evren. At the end of his visit, a joint communiqué was published, which at first was little more than a repetition of the statements made in May. But then new tones followed: it was intended to set up a sub-committee to revise the textbooks of both countries. Furthermore, a paper was signed that contained guidelines for the prevention of accidents and incidents on the high seas and in international airspace. According to this, Greek and Turkish naval units were to refrain from pursuing each other on the high seas in future. During manoeuvres, the respective surveillance units were to keep such a distance that the manoeuvre would not be disturbed. With regard to airspace, the paper stated that *"pilots of Greek and Turkish aircraft will act in conformity with international law! and shall display utmost caution when in the proximity of aircraft of the other party and shall not manoeuvre or react in a manner that would be hazardous to the safety of the flight and/or affect the conduct of the mission of the aircraft ... to promote the climate of confidence, whenever there are claims of acts contrary to the above, the two sides will inform each other through diplomatic channels prior to releasing official statements"*.

It was planned to hold another meeting of the political committee in early 1989, the tasks of which would be determined by the two prime ministers. Both sides were satisfied with the outcome of the meeting: it had been possible not only to strengthen the confidence-building measures but even to expand them. The spirit of Davos was alive and well and the two sides were looking to the future with confidence.[2]

The results of the meeting of the economic committee were less spectacular but quite concrete. In October, expert talks were to begin on an agreement to avoid double taxation. Negotiations on a maritime transport agreement were to begin in November. A joint investment bank was to be established as soon as possible, with the help of which the issues of Greek property in Turkey in particular were to be solved. Experts should also negotiate cooperation in road and rail transport. Further cooperation was agreed for the tourism, trade, air transport and building construction sectors.[3]

The negotiations of the two committees had thus made substantial progress in improving relations between Ankara and Athens. Now it would have been important to follow the upco-

---

1 *Athens News Agency*, 6. September 1988.
"The fact that Greece is trying to link the Cyprus problem to the process started in Davos is an example. Greece is now claiming that some of the issues it originally agreed to discuss touch on national sovereignty and are non-negotiable".

2 *Athens News Agency, 9. September 1988.*
"The pilots of Greek and Turkish aircraft will behave in accordance with the rules of international law and, when in the vicinity of an aircraft of the other side, will exercise the utmost caution and will not manoeuvre or react in any way that would be risky for the safety of the flight or detrimental to the execution of the aircraft's mission.... Should any actions allegedly contradict the above occur, both sides, before making official statements, will inform each other through diplomatic channels in order to promote the climate of confidence".

3 *Athens News Agency*, 8. September 1988.

ming inter-communal talks in Cyprus and to promote them at the decisive moment through appropriate means via Ankara, so that they would also produce concrete, presentable results. But this is precisely what Athens was unable to do over the next few weeks. Three events practically paralysed Greek politics for weeks: Papandreou's heart operation, his affair with the former stewardess, Dimitra Liani, and the Koskotas scandal. Although the meetings of the subordinate bodies agreed in Ankara and Athens took place, Athens was not in a position to pursue an active Cyprus policy.

Athens' passivity on this issue was registered in Ankara and since there were also domestic problems there (referendum, Iraqi Kurds, inflation) that absorbed Ozal's attention, he did not give the inter-communal dialogue the attention it deserved. In addition, the EC had given Ankara to understand that an enlargement of the community would not be considered until 1993 at the earliest. Ankara was therefore under no immediate pressure to act. Denktash registered this development very carefully and seized his opportunity.

The new round of intercommunal talks began as scheduled on 15 September. Vassiliou and Denktash met under the chairmanship of Camillion at the Ledra Hotel on the demarcation line. In the press conference that followed, Camillion said that the task ahead of them was difficult but favoured by the international climate of detente. Vassiliou stressed that he did not underestimate the difficulties ahead and did not want to raise false hopes of a quick solution. *"We must try harder than ever before and our efforts must not aim at how to score victories against each other, but at how to win together a new Cyprus where all its inhabitants will live and work in peace and prosperity ... If we are to save Cyprus at this moment of grave peril we must rid ourselves of bitter memories of the past and admit frankly that nobody is infallible ... The tools for repairing the edifice of Cyprus should be tolerance, sincerety, understanding, trust and abundance of goodwill. We are experiencing a peace epidemie. Let us hope that Cyprus will also benefit."*

Denktasch expressed a similarly positive view: "When we talk about the past, we do not do this in order to fill ourselves with anger or iII feelings against the Greek Cypriots, but in order to build a future which will not repeat the mistakes of the past ... Let us move forward with goodwill, and try to understand each other's fears and apprehensions. Let us make Cyprus aland of two people who have differences of religion, language, national identity and culture, but have one and the same loyalty to Cyprus. Let us work for final peac".[1]

Both sides agreed on strict confidentiality of the talks. Information to the press would be passed on by the UN in written form. This agreement was largely adhered to, so that hardly any information is available on the content of the negotiations. However, since these did not make any substantial progress, as became apparent in the course of the following weeks, some

1 *Athens News Agency,* 16. September 1988.
We must strive harder than ever before and our efforts must not be aimed at achieving victories over each other but at how we can win together a new Cyprus in which all the inhabitants live and work in peace and prosperity.... If we are to save Cyprus from the present great danger, we must free ourselves from the bitter memories of the past and openly admit that no one is infallible. The tools to restore Cyprus should be tolerance, seriousness, understanding, trust and an abundance of goodwill. We are currently experiencing a peace epidemic. Let us hope that Cyprus will also benefit from it".
"When we talk about the past, we do so not to fill ourselves with anger or hatred towards Greek Cypriots, but to build a future in which the mistakes of the past are not repeated ... Let us approach this with goodwill and try to understand the fears and anxieties on both sides. Let us make Cyprus one country with two peoples who, although they have different religions, languages, national identities and cultures, nevertheless share a common loyalty to Cyprus. Let us strive for peace."

developments in the background will be analysed instead, which at the same time also allow some conclusions to be drawn about the negotiations themselves.

One of the most striking differences in the behaviour of the two negotiators was that Vassiliou informed the Greek Cypriot party leaders within the framework of the National Council about the content and course of the negotiations. Denktash, on the other hand, only informed his "government", which led to strong complaints from the opposition parties. The involvement of the opposition in the South went far beyond mere information, which became visible when Glafkos Kliridis met with Yilmaz in Rhodes for a discussion lasting several hours within the framework of the European Democratic Union Conference and gained the impression that the intercommunal talks could lead to a solution. Although there were also different opinions in the South about the sense of the negotiation, e.g. Kyprianou' and Lyssaridis were in favour of a tougher course, one can nevertheless speak of a kind of consensus. In the North, on the other hand, there was a kind of game with divided roles. In the first phase, Denktash was conciliatory, whereas his "prime minister", Eroglou, played the role of the hardliner, whereby it can be assumed that he only said what was in Denktash's interest.

Parallel to the talks between Vassiliou and Denktash, the Cypriot government continued to seek international support. To this end, Foreign Minister lakovou flew to the UN General Assembly in New York at the end of September. There, on 27 September, Foreign Minister Papoulias, in his capacity as Chairman of the EC Council of Foreign Ministers, gave a speech. in which he stressed, among other things, that the European Community wanted a just Cyprus solution. He then stressed. "We stand fully by our previous statements and reject any action which purports to establish an independent state within Cyprus."[1] A day later, Papoulias spoke with Perez de Cuellar about the intercommunal dialogue. This was followed by talks with Yilmaz and lakovou on 29 September. lakovou held talks with US Secretary of State Shultz on the same day, with Secretary of State Ridgeway and James Wilkinson present.

At the beginning of October there was a pause in the inter-communal negotiations, which Vassiliou used to seek international support for himself. On 4 October he arrived in London for talks with Mrs Thatcher. It was later learned that Mrs. Thatcher showed great interest and expressed her hope for a speedy solution. On 6 October, Vassiliou addressed the UN General Assembly in New York. On 7 October, Vassiliou flew to Paris. On 10 October, after a meeting with Vassiliou, President Mitterrand stressed that the French government supported the efforts to reach a settlement in Cyprus. France recognised only one president, only one government and only one state in Cyprus. Apart from Turkey, no state recognised the secessionist state of the North. With regard to a possible application by Cyprus to join the EC, Mitterrand said that France would consider such an application very favourably.[2] On the 11th, head of government Rocard assured that France wanted to play a more active and creative role in the solution of the Cyprus problem.

Mitterand's statements infuriated Denktash. In an interview with the Northern Cyprus Radio, he berated Mitterand in the strongest terms and then criticised Vassiliou: *"Unfortunately in the space of three to five weeks, Mr. Vassiliou has put on Kyprianou's shoes. I thought that we could establish a gbod dialogue. However, responsibility for this negative development, is not solely with Vassiliou. All the countries which are spoiling the usurper Greek Cy-*

1 *Athens News Agency,* 28. September 1988.
"We stand fully by our previous statements and reject any action aimed at establishing an independent state within Cyprus".

2 *Athens News Agency*, 10 October 1988

priot administration have a share in it." Denktasch continued: *"What is the use of continuing the talks? How long do they think we will let them make fun of the Turkish Cypriots? The UN Secretary General should openly and clearly announce that he disapproves this action which is contrary to his line of action. The UN Secretary Genral should warn the countries wfiich treat the Greek Cypriots in such a way that it is tantamount to saying to the Greeks that it is right to colonize the Turkish Cypriots by force of arms".*

Denktash then accused Vassiliou of torpedoing the intercommunal talks. Vassiliou's actions had completely desitlusionier him roo. Vassiliou responded to these accusations by stating on Cypriot television that the talks in London. New York and Paris had been set when there was no talk of intercommunal negotiations. The opposition RTP organ Yeniduzen said on 17 October that Vassiliou's statements only gave the forces in the north a convenient excuse to break off the talks.

Nevertheless, the talks were resumed on 17 October and continued on 18 October. Denktash was again quite diplomatic, but his "prime minister" polemicised for this in a press conference: "1 believe that at some point we will be forced to tell the Greek Cypriots to choose between the negotiation table or the continuation of their policy of international deception. Those countries that are friends of Cyprus must frankly close the doors of unilateral contact with Vassiliou during the intercommunal talks if they do not want us to reach this point. With these visits, Vassiliou has violated the Geneva agreement. If he continues to violate the Geneva agreement, the talks with the Greek Cypriots will be useless." Opposition leader özker Özgür then accused the NUP government of working against a federal solution. They forced the village elders to sign an open letter to Denktash demanding that he make no further concessions.[1] The mainland newspaper Milliyet got the impression that the reason the talks were continuing was because neither side wanted to be the first to leave the conference table. The negotiations would continue, but would not produce results.[2]

The first round of talks ended on 7 November. Nothing was made public about the results. But there were accompanying circumstances that suggested that the positions had hardly converged.

In September, the Vice-President of the Conservative Party (DHSY), Giannakis Matsis, had sent an invitation via Camillion to two specific MPs each from the NUP, the CLP and the RTP. The purpose of the visit was to promote mutual understanding. The CLP and RTP MPs accepted. On 3 November, the NUP announced on Northern Cyprus Radio that it was refusing the "propaganda" invitation. At the same time, it was announced that the Soviet ambassador

---

1 Quoted from Cyprus -Ministry of Interior -Press and Information Office -*Turhish Press and Other Media,* Nr. 244/88 of 15 October 1988.

"Unfortunately, Mr Vassiliou has managed to acquire Kyprianou's behaviour within a period of three to five weeks. I believed that we could start a good conversation. However, the responsibility for this negative development does not lie solely with Mr Vassiliou. All countries that approve of the behaviour of the usurpist Greek Cypriot government are involved ... What is the point of continuing the talks? How long do they think we Turkish Cypriots will be fooled. The UN Secretary General should clearly announce that he disapproves of this action which is contrary to his intentions. The UN Secretary General should caution those countries who treated the Greek Cypriots as if they were saying to them that it is right to colonise the Turkish Cypriots by force of arms. I believe that the time will come when we will have to tell the Greek Cypriots that they have to choose between the negotiating table and the continuation of their policy of deceiving the public. Those countries that consider themselves friends of Cyprus must close the door to unilateral contacts with Vassiliou for the duration of the intercommunal talks if they do not want us to do so. Vassiliou has violated the Geneva Agreement with these talks. If he continues, the talks with the Greek Cypriots will be useless."

2 Milliyet, 20. Oktober 1988

would give a reception on 7 November to mark the 71st anniversary of the October Revolution, to which representatives of the Turkish Cypriot parties were also invited. Representatives of the RTP had applied to the "Foreign Ministry" to leave the country.

Denktash reacted irritably to this request: The "border" between the "TRNC" and South Cyprus has a meaning. It is not a line that anyone could cross at will for private purposes. Until the Cyprus problem is solved, the border has a meaning and is the symbol of the existence of the TRNC. The Soviet Union had been asked to provide a reception in the north, which had been refused. People who crossed the border to the south were against the Turkish side. If they did so, they would have to bear the consequences. Commenting on the talks with Vassiliou, Denktash said that they had not gone beyond taking stock and discussing principles for a solution. He concluded by accusing the EC of discriminating against the "TRNC" when it hands over aid funds to the South for distribution.[1]

Those attacked defended themselves. CLP leader Mustafa Akinci said Denktash's attacks were only meant to smear the opposition. The editorial in the CLP newspaper, Ortam, countered that anyone who goes to talks with Greek Cypriots is denounced by the regime as a "sell-out" and anyone who accepts such invitations is branded a "traitor". The ones who were actually taking a risk were the Greek Cypriots. After all, they had invited NUP representatives and no one would stop them from speaking their minds.[2] Özker Ozgür accused Denktash and the NUP of being afraid that an intercommunal rapport would endanger the authority of the regime. Any contact between the two communities at any level would cause panic and the regime would try to torpedo the rapprochement and create the impression that the end of the world was coming.[3]

The four MPs appeared at the "border" on 7 November, which they crossed after being photographed by Turkish officials. They then held talks with Lyssaridis, Kliridis, Kyprianou and representatives of AKEL. In the evening, Vassiliou received the four MPs. Later they went to the reception of the Soviet ambassador, to which Akinci and Ozgür also attended. This led to talks with Vassiliou, who also attended the reception. Further talks with Greek Cypriot politicians took place on the 8th and they returned to the North the next day. The Greek Cypriot side was very satisfied with the visit. During the discussion on possible solutions, they discovered differences but also many common approaches. The four Turkish Cypriots told the press that their visit was an important step towards creating mutual understanding, goodwill and peaceful contacts. Such contacts should take place more often.[4]

Even before the return of the four, "Prime Minister" Eroglou threatened consequences on the radio, stating that a return of the Greek Cypriot refugees to their homeland within the framework of a bi-zonal solution was out of the question. "Foreign Minister" Atakol added that holding on to the three freedoms made a solution to the Cyprus problem impossible. There were no concessions on the Turkish Cypriot side on this issue. Özgür then accused Denktash and his NUP of using the visit of the four as a pretext to torpedo the intercommunal talks. In fact, they did not want any concrete results at all. These were methods of a racist and fascist nature. Akinci criticised Denktash for denouncing the well-wishers as traitors instead of par-

1 Cyprus -Ministry of the Interior -Press and Information Office -*Turkish Press and Other Media,* Nr. 267/88 on on 5 November 1988

2 *Ortam,* 5 November 1988.

3 Yeniduzen, 7 November 1988.

4 *Athens News Agency*, 10. November 1988.

ticipating in the rapprochement process. On 11 November, NUP MPs massively attacked the four oppositionists in the Northern Cypriot National Assembly. One of them, CLP MP Ismail Bozkurt, defended himself: Denktash could have benefited from their visit by exchanging ideas with the opposition so shortly before the talks in New York. But this opportunity had been squandered.

Vassiliou had meanwhile flown to Rome for a working visit. After extensive talks with Italian politicians from all parties, who assured him of their support, Vassiliou flew to Brussels. At a joint press conference with Cheysson, the latter stated that the Cyprus problem was not a Greek-Turkish dispute but directly concerned the EC, which could not accept the illegal presence of Turkish occupation forces in the north of the island. This was followed by talks with Belgian Prime Minister Martens, who explained that his country had had similar problems to Cyprus and that they had been solved in a democratic way. On 16 November, Vassiliou assured himself of the support of the government of Luxembourg. He returned to Nicosia on 17 November. Foreign Minister lakovou, who had accompanied him, went to Athens to brief the Greek government on the results of the intercommunal talks and the way forward. On 18 November, Vassiliou informed the cabinet and the National Council of the development and invited the party leaders to accompany him to New York for the talks with de Cuellar and Denktash. Kliridis and Christofias (AKEL) accepted. Kyprianou and Lyssaridis declined, saying that their presence would create a false impression.

Meanwhile, in the north, preparations were being made for the five-year anniversary of the proclamation of the "TRNC". On 13 November, former Prime Minister Bulent Ecevit spoke out: if the intercommunal talks did not produce results, Turkey should make efforts to have the "TRNC" recognised. On the evening of the same day, Minister of State Abdullah T Enekeci appeared as Turkey's official representative at the celebrations in Cyprus. At the joint press conference with Denktash, it was noticeable that Tenekeci expressed himself very reservedly. Foreign Minister Yilmaz also expressed himself in a very moderate manner before the parliament in Ankara: Turkey fully adheres to the agreements made with Athens and expects Athens to do the same. The Cyprus conflict would be solved by the establishment of a bi-zonal, bicommunal federation on the basis of equal rights for the two peoples on the island. On 14 November, Denktash briefed MPs on the latest development in a closed session. Afterwards, he claimed that full consensus had been reached.

On 15 November, the weekly Gunaydin Kibris published a long interview with Denktash in which he critically discussed Ecevit's policies in the years after 1975 and accused him of trying to depose him, Denktash. Turning to the present, Denktash stated that even if an agreement was reached with the Greek side, the "TRNC" would not be dissolved. The federation would consist of two states. Should the negotiations be broken off, efforts would be made to have the "TRNC" recognised. The time was ripe for this.

Denktash's statements clearly showed that he was aiming at a confederation solution and was only looking for a pretext to torpedo it himself. What purpose Denktash was pursuing with his revelations about Ecevit is not so clear. Was it to avenge past violations or was it to put pressure on the Özal government to follow his course?

On the same day, Arafat proclaimed the Palestinian state in Algiers. Denktash immediately tried to exploit the recognition in his favour. Before leaving for talks in Ankara, he told reporters that he would ask the Turkish government to support him in a campaign to recognise the "TRNC". He said he had no doubt that Ankara had already taken steps to that effect. Recognition would not block the road to federation, but would make it easier, as it would show the Greeks that they had no claim to sole representation.

On his arrival at the Ankara airport, where he was received by Yilmaz and Tenekeci, he said in an interview that he expected the Islamic world to recognise not only the Palestinian state but also its "TRNC". At the very least, the Islamic world must respect the fact that there are two equal zones in Cyprus. Official recognition as a state would be perfectly compatible with the plans for a federation. The Turkish government reacted coolly to Denktash's demands. The spokesman of the Foreign Ministry, Inal Batu, did not say a word about Denktash's demands, but only repeated the familiar formulas.

According to a report in Hurriyet on 19 November, President Evren was allegedly in favour of Denktash's proposals. However, Foreign Minister Yilmaz had blocked the idea: as long as the talks continued, recognition was out of the question. Obviously, Yilmaz wanted to avoid a breakdown of the upcoming talks.

On 21 and 22 November, the planned talks between Vassiliou, Denktash and de Cuellar took place. On the 23rd it was agreed that the intercommunal talks would continue on 19 December in Nicosia. This second round of talks was to clarify the positions of both sides on those issues that constituted the Cyprus conflict. At the same time, options should be developed which would be examined in the light of mutual interests and concerns. In the first half of March, they would meet again with de Cuellar, who would then initiate the third round of negotiations on the basis of the proposals developed by then. This ensured that the intercommunal talks would continue, despite a surprise coup by Denktash the day before.

On 22 November, Denktash had announced new "creative" proposals to solve the Cyprus problem: the Greek side was making difficulties in connection with the three freedoms. Therefore, he presented concrete proposals that would prove the good will on his side. Denktash presented his "creative" proposals to de Cueilar . On the grounds that they had met to clarify procedural questions, the proposals were not discussed on the 23rd.

Although confidentiality had been agreed upon, the main content of Denktash's proposals became known as late as the 22nd through a report from New York on Turkish radio. On 3 December, the details of the proposals were published on Northern Cyprus Radio. According to these, Denktash saw the solution to the Cyprus question in the creation of the "United Republics of Cyprus". The "Turkish Republic of Northern Cyprus" ("TRNCO) and the "Greek Republic of Southern Cyprus" were to form two separate and equal states of the federation, which were to be sovereign in their internal affairs. The "Three Freedoms" were to be included in the catalogue of fundamental rights of the future constitution. But then followed some serious restrictions. Among other things, the police of the two republics were to have the right to expel undesirable persons from the territory of the respective republic. Before the right of free settlement could be exercised, a moratorium period of 18 years would have to pass. However, it would be possible to revise this provision nine years after the beginning of the moratorium.

After the beginning of the moratorium, both republics were to determine the maximum number of Turkish and Greek Cypriots they were willing to accept as settlers. This maximum number could be fixed either for the territory of the whole Republic or for certain regions.

With regard to the right to property, Denktash's proposal provided for the following: Property claims from before 1974 should be satisfied by a joint commission before the establishment of the federation, either by restitution or by compensation. After that, there would also be a moratorium of 18 years on property claims. After this period, the respective constituent republic would regulate the right to property with a view to protecting its character.

The proposal then addressed the armed forces of the republics, which would have to be organised separately and form a balance together with the contingents of the mother countries.

In the next round of inter-communal talks, the constitutional principles and structures of the new state would have to be discussed and determined. No progress could be made unless agreement was reached on the political equality of the two constituent states and the two peoples in all organs of government. The Turkish Cypriot side was striving for the establishment of a bicommunal and bi-zonal federal republic. But such a federation could only be achieved on the basis of the present situation. The proposals formed a package and could only be accepted as a whole.

The proposals show that Denktash was by no means aiming for a federal solution, but was still striving for a loose confederation of two largely sovereign states. His proposal to suspend the right of free settlement and the right to property until at least 2006 proves that he wants to cement the status quo. When he made these proposals, it must have been clear to him that the moratoria would be unacceptable to the Greek Cypriot side. This suggests that Denktash was out to provoke the other side into breaking off the negotiations. But this was precisely what was avoided by the restrained reaction of de Cuellar and Vassilious. And since the Athenian press was fully occupied with the Koskotas scandal, Denktash's proposals did not even make headlines there.

In the following days, Denktash repeatedly tried to prove his willingness to compromise with his proposals. But since only fragments were known, practically only the Turkish and Turkish-Cypriot press were interested in his statements. In his efforts to gain recognition, Denktash always tried to give the impression that he represented the views of the Turkish Cypriots. The opposition, however, had quite different ideas.

On 25 November, Özker özgür spoke about the Cyprus problem at an RTP meeting in Morphou. Turkey must remain one of the guarantors of the future Federal Republic of Cyprus, but he would prefer the UN Security Council to be added to the three traditional guarantors. The mutual mistrust between the two communities must be taken into account in the search for a solution. The problem of ownership could be solved by a joint commission under the leadership of UN experts. Once the property issue was resolved, the problem of the three freedoms could be easily solved. For this, however, it is necessary to have a positive effect on the attitude of the youth.

The Turkish settlers, with the exception of those who had married Turkish Cypriots, had to return to their homeland. The whole island must be demilitarised and the British bases closed. In return, a precisely defined number of Greek and Turkish military units should remain in Cyprus. The policy of the NUP is to maintain the status quo. Making peace is more difficult than waging war. He therefore appealed to Denktash and Vassiliou to behave constructively.

On 25 November, Vassiliou flew to Athens via London, where he informed Mrs. Thatcher of the results of the New York talks. After the meeting with Papandreou, he assured her that he would raise the Cyprus problem at the forthcoming EC summit in Rhodes. The leader of the conservative Nea Dimokratia. Konstantinos Mitsotakis, declared after a conversation with Vassiliou that despite all domestic political differences in Greece, there was unity on the Cyprus issue. Vassiliou returned to Cyprus on 28 November.

After the conclusion of the talks in New York, there was also renewed movement in international politics. On 27 November, a group of members of the US House of Representatives and the Soviet Union's Deputy Minister of the Interior, Ivan Shilov, arrived in Nicosia to learn about the situation in Cyprus. Both sides assured on their departure that they supported a just solution to Cyprus.

On 28 November, Özal became the first Turkish prime minister to visit Paris after 17 years of diplomatic tension. At the Elysee Palace, it was emphasised that a period of tension caused by the invasion of Cyprus and Turkey's disregard for human rights had come to an end. During the talks, Mitterrand and Özal discussed bilateral problems, the desire for EC accession and the Cyprus problem. At the concluding press conference, Özal announced that after the successful conclusion of the inter-communal talks, Turkish troops would of course be withdrawn from Cyprus.[1] It was unlikely that Paris would have agreed to the normalisation of relations if Ankara had not previously made any concrete commitments on the human rights and Cyprus question.

On 29 November, Foreign Minister Yilmaz commented on the "Davos Process" in the Turkish Parliament: It was pointless to accuse Greece of intransigence. There is no alternative to the "Davos Process". The current difficulties in bilateral relations are not due to the complexity of the problems, but to the fact that they are not being solved. Yi!maz then listed the problems and said it was time to get down to solving them.[2]

On 1 December, the EC summit began in Rhodes. On the very first day it produced an important result for Cyprus. Foreign Minister Papoulias, in his capacity as Chairman of the EC Council of Foreign Ministers, opened the first official talks between the EC and Cyprus with Foreign Minister lakovou. From now on, such talks should take place every six months.

At the dinner on 2 December, Papandreou informed the other heads of government about the latest developments in the Cyprus problem. If the talks had not made progress, it was due to Turkish intransigence. The Turkish Cypriot leader has not moved away from his extreme positions on any of the key issues. He still insists that Turkish troops must remain in Cyprus even after a settlement and the establishment of a joint government. He denied the presence of over 60,000 settlers. He wants a constitution in which the minority has the same weight as the majority. Finally, he does not respect fundamental freedoms. In conclusion, Papandreou remarked: *"I think that it is imperative to persuade Turkey that the only viable and lasting solution to the problem is to bring about a genuinely independent and united Republic of Cyprus, and not a Cyprus as conceived by Mr Denktasch, which is partitioned and under military occupation. This message must be understood by the Turkish side, and I therefore would ask for your support to this end in order that the rule of law and not the rule of might should once again prevail in Cyprus".*

On 4 December, the Cyprus question was subsequently included in the final resolution of the Twelve: "The European Council had a discussion of the Cyprus problem. It acknowledged the fact that the tragic division of the island remains unchanged and reaffirmed the previous declarations of the Twelve, which support without any reservation the independence, sovereignty, territorial integrity and unity of Cyprus. While expressing its satisfaction at the resumption of the intercommunal dialogue, the European Council expressed the wish that this dialogue should progress and lead rapidly to a solution of the problem, on the basis of the above principles and the relevant UN resolutions.[3]

---

1 *Athens News Agency,* 1,. December 1988.

2 *Athens News Agency,* 30 November 1988.

3 Athens News Agency, *Focus on the News: The European Council Rhodes, December* 2 -3, 1988, Nr. 8, 12. Dezember 1988.

"I believe that there is an urgent need to convince Turkey that the only feasible and lasting solution to the problem is to create a truly independent and united Republic of Cyprus and not a Cyprus that is divided and militarily occupied as Mr Denktash envisages. This message must be understood by the Turkish side and therefore I would like to ask you to support this objective so that the law and not violence again prevails in

On 7 December, the Soviet Union spoke out. In a paper handed over to the UN in New York, the Soviet Union again called for the convening of an international conference to resolve the international aspects of the Cyprus problem. The Turkish Cypriot leadership, supported by Ankara, rejected such a conference and believed that it could disregard UN resolutions. A partition of Cyprus, in whatever form, is unacceptable. Cyprus must be demilitarised, all military contingents of other countries withdrawn and foreign military bases closed. The inter-communal talks should solve the internal problems. The international aspects, such as withdrawal of foreign troops, repatriation of settlers and guarantees, should be solved at an international conference under the auspices of the UN.[1] Nicosia welcomed the Soviet proposal. Ankara was disgruntled.

A day later, Reagan welcomed the efforts to find a Cyprus solution. On 5 December, a new Cypriot ambassador to Algiers was appointed. On 12 December, Iran and Cyprus established diplomatic relations. On the 17th, it was announced that Libya and Cyprus would exchange ambassadors within a short time. Denktash's hope for Islamic solidarity in favour of the "TRNC" had proved illusory.

Finally, on 19 December, negotiations began on the second round of intercommunal talks. The day before, in a speech in Paphos, Vassiliou had shared his thoughts on the second round of talks: it was the first time since the invasion of Cyprus that foreign governments were actually interested in Cyprus and wanted progress in the talks. To this end, these governments were also putting pressure on Turkey. They were trying to convince Ankara that a withdrawal from Cyprus would also benefit Turkey. The idea that the talks would put pressure on the Greek Cypriot side and force it to make concessions is wrong. The opposite is the case. If there are no talks, there is no hope that pressure will be put on the other side. Only by continuing the talks could it be shown that the other side was intransigent. A breakdown of the talks would be fatal.[2] The talks between Vassiliou, Denktash and Camillion were again of a procedural nature. It was agreed that the actual negotiations would begin on 9 January 1989.

On the same day that the intercommunal talks resumed, an unpleasant event occurred. Opposition leader Özker Özgür had invited Greek Cypriot journalists to a press conference in North Nicosia. When the 17 journalists appeared at the "border" north of the Ledra Palace Hotel, the border police officers demanded that they fill out an application for permission to enter the "NTRNC" and sign it. The journalists refused to sign, saying that this constituted a form of recognition of the "TRNC", whereupon they were refused entry. Clearly, the regime was trying to prevent the opposition's views on the Cyprus problem from becoming known.

Despite these obstacles, Ögür's views reached the South. He called on the Greek Cypriots to respond to Denktash's proposals. It was clear from them what importance the Turkish Cypriots attached to political equality. If the Greek Cypriots were to accommodate the Turkish Cypriot side on this issue, this would lead to more flexibility on other fundamental aspects of the Cyprus problem. If the principle of bi-zonality and bi-communality, as described in previous agreements, were actually accepted, the current stagnation could be overcome. Özgür

---

Cyprus." "The European Council discussed the Cyprus problem. It took note of the fact that the tragic division of the island still continues unchanged and reaffirmed the earlier Declaration of the Twelve, which supports without any qualification the independence, sovereignty, territorial integrity and unity of Cyprus. While welcoming the resumption of the inter-communal talks, he expressed his wish that this dialogue make progress and lead rapidly to a solution of the problem on the basis of the above principles and related UN resolutions".

1 *Athens News Agency* 8 December 1988.

2 *Athens News Agency,* 20. December 1988.

then criticised Denktash for his negative stance on the intercommunal talks and his position that the status quo was a solution to the conflict. This, he said, puts Ankara in a very difficult position internationally.[1]

On 21 December, Foreign Minister Yilmaz made a statement in the Turkish Parliament. He welcomed Papandreou's visit to Ankara, scheduled for February. It was expected that during this visit the two prime ministers would open the way to substantive talks on the bilateral problems and to permanent solutions. The agreements reached so far are useful, but now it is necessary to move towards solutions. The current difficulty is not that the problems at hand are too complicated, but that they are not discussed.

As far as Cyprus is concerned, there are certain preconditions for the withdrawal of Turkish troops. If these conditions are met, Turkey will withdraw its troops. However, withdrawal is out of the question as long as the security of the Turkish Cypriots is not guaranteed. If the Greek side stops arming itself and reduces the number of its troops, it will react accordingly. A just and lasting solution could only be found on the basis of equal rights for the two communities in a bi-zonal federation. He hoped that the Greek Cypriot side would react constructively to Denktash's proposals, which had the full support of the Turkish government.[2]

Yilmaz's remarks contained some new elements, but his statement that Ankara supports Denktash's proposals raises scepticism. Yilmaz did speak of a federation. Did he really mean a federal republic or did he not support Denktash's confederation model of the United Republics of Cyprus on this issue? As long as Ankara did not clearly define the term "federation", - scepticism would be in order for some time to come.

Not a word was heard from Athens about the resumption of inter-communal talks. There, the crisis that had been going on since the summer of 1988 had reached a climax: the government was threatening to fall. As long as this crisis was not overcome, Athens would be able to contribute little to the solution of Cyprus. It will be even less able to solve the bilateral problems through a compromise. A compromise will always be unpopular, and how can an ailing government facing elections find the courage to do so?

Fortunately, the international community has put the Cyprus question on the list of problems to be solved, so that there is some hope that a solution can still be found in Cyprus in 1989, despite Athens' default. The solution of the Greek-Turkish conflict, on the other hand, is likely to be put on hold until after the Greek elections, unless a miracle happens during Papandreou's visit to Ankara.

---

1 *Athens News Agency,* 21 December 1988.
2 *Athens News Agency,* 22 December 1988.

However, if one looks at the sub-conflicts that constitute it, different degrees of progress towards resolution can be identified. The bilateral Greek-Turkish conflict has progressed beyond the state of "'non-war'" to the process of creating confidence-building measures and cooperation in "non-political" fields. But the actual points of conflict have not even been discussed. In this respect, the solution of the Cyprus conflict has progressed further. In the meantime, concrete solutions are being sought there.

At the same time, the character of the conflicts underwent fundamental changes, most clearly that of the Cyprus conflict, and less markedly that of the Aegean conflict. The tri--lateral Cyprus conflict (Cyprus, Greece, Turkey), in which third powers were only moderately interested despite all the numerous declarations and resolutions to the contrary, became one of those conflicts in which the superpowers are trying to find a solution within the framework of global detente. However, the willingness of the superpowers to resolve the conflict is less pronounced in the Cyprus conflict than in other conflict hotspots where they themselves are involved. Therefore, the EC's involvement takes on a much greater weight, especially since both Turkey and Cyprus have the desire to become EC members.

The importance to be attached to the European Community's involvement in the Cyprus question became clearly visible when Athens, because of the permanent domestic crisis since the summer of 1988, was only partially able to play its traditional role as international promoter of Cyprus and the EC took over this role. The Europeans made it clear to Ankara that before the Cyprus conflict could be resolved according to their ideas and Turkey's respect for human rights, which would require a fundamental change in Turkey's minority policy, even a rapprochement of Ankara with Europe was out of the question.

It is clear that Ankara will attach greater weight to the increasing commitment of the EC states than to Athens' previous efforts, which were easier to play down propagandistically as exaggerated demands of Athens' eccentric politics. The decisive question, however, is whether the Europeans are really prepared to accept Turkey as an EC member in the foreseeable future or whether they are playing a Machiavellian game and either using a failure of the Cyprus solution as a pretext or using Greece's possibility of a veto as an alibi to keep Turkey out of the EC. While such a manoeuvre is not yet on the horizon, given the fears of some European countries of an uncontrolled influx of hundreds of thousands of Turkish guest workers, it is not entirely out of the question. Both Athens and Nicosia should not ignore this aspect in their EC policies. It is clear, however, that the EC states can contribute more to the solution of the Cyprus conflict than the Western European public has so far been aware of.

In contrast to the Cyprus conflict, the bilateral Aegean conflict has hardly been "internationalised" or "Europeanised". Neither NATO nor the EC have so far shown any inclination to intervene in this dispute. The Islamic Revolution in Iran (1979), the Soviet invasion of Afghanistan (1979), the Gulf War (1980), the Israeli invasion of Lebanon (1982) caused Turkey's strategic importance to rise unexpectedly in the eyes of the Reagan administration. External signs of this were the modernisation of the US installations in Turkey (1982) and the constant attempts of the Reagan administration to change the legally anchored 7:10 ratio in favour of Turkey against the will of Congress. In addition, the Turkish generals constantly proved to be compliant allies who also effectively fought Reagan's main enemy, terrorism (communism).

The left-wing PASOK ruling in Athens filled the US administration with deep suspicion, jealously guarding Greek sovereignty and repeatedly threatening to close US bases in the face of real or imagined violations of it. In the eyes of the Reagan administration, these were attempts to humiliate the . USA. It is little wonder, therefore, that the US administration turned a deaf ear to Greek demands for guarantees against an attack from the east, cared little for the legal dispute over the shelf and left the settlement of the Cyprus dispute to the UN Secretary General; knowing full well that he alone would achieve little. This was despite the fact that the USA itself had been instrumental in creating the problem in the past. Only recently (after Vassiliou's visit to Washington) has there been a somewhat greater interest on the part of the USA in the Cyprus conflict. But the international conference proposed by Gorbachev is still rejected by Washington (as well as by Ankara). The solution of the Aegean conflict is thus left to Ankara and Athens for the time being.

But it is precisely in bilateral relations that a radical change has taken place, fuelling the hope that the Aegean conflict can also be resolved. For years, both sides avoided dialogue and at best had indirect contacts through NATO channels or via the USA. The shock of the March crisis of 1987 initiated a process of rethinking. On both sides, the decisive statesmen are in favour of rapprochement. But there are also forces on both sides that observe the reconciliation process with suspicion, want to maintain the status quo or even continue the traditional course of confrontation.

On the Turkish side, Prime Minister Özal seems determined to end the conflict with Greece. The motives guiding him are of a complex foreign and domestic political nature: One point that is not given much attention in the analysis from a European perspective is the desire of Özal and the Turkish military to modernise the country's armed forces. Due to a lack of foreign currency, this can only be done through American and allied military aid. However, American military aid has been fixed by Congress at the 7:10 ratio. The Reagan administration constantly tried to circumvent this regulation, but was regularly prevented from doing so by Congress, due to the influence of the extremely efficient Greek lobby in Congress. A change in the attitude of Congress on this issue can therefore only be expected if Özal succeeds in convincing the Greek lobby of his peaceful intentions towards Greece and Cyprus.

On the other hand, Ozal fears Islamic fundamentalism (even if he occasionally flirts with the fundamentalists for reasons of coalition arithmetic), which could also overrun Turkey and threaten the secular state created by Kemal Atatürk. This fear is also shared by the Turkish army, which, as is well known, sees itself as the guardian of Kemalism. Özal can therefore certainly count on the support of the military in his defence against fundamentalism.

Özal's concept for warding off the fundamentalist danger is, strictly speaking, the same as Atatürk's. He wants to make Turkey a European country. Özal knows that the EC is more than sceptical about Turkey joining the Community. He is also aware that without a settlement of the Cyprus conflict and an end to the bilateral Greek-Turkish conflict, the Europeans are not even prepared to start preliminary talks. Before he can normalise relations with Europe, this regional conflict must be resolved.

He knows that in addition to the general European concerns, Athens will veto Turkey's EC accession unless the overall conflict is resolved first. The Turkish side occasionally argues that a solution to the conflict would be easier if Turkey were first admitted to the Community and then the conflict was resolved within the Community. But the intention behind this argumentation is transparent: Ankara would still try to solve the Aegean conflict in its own way. The community will be careful not to increase its internal difficulties immeasurably through this conflict. And Athens will hardly be willing to give up its only trump card in the poker game for the resolution of the conflict.

Özal's motives for joining the EC are not limited to the defence against fundamentalism. He and the rest of the Turkish ruling elite, both civilian and military, dream of making Turkey a power factor in the Middle East region, not only in military terms but also in economic and political terms. This long-term goal can also only be achieved with Europe's help.

Another motive is likely to be the growing difficulties of the Turkish economy, exacerbated by the burden of financing the "TRNC". Another aspect is Özal's attempt to strengthen the civilian government and prevent future interventions by the army, a policy similar to that of Greece after 1974. The impact of international pressure should also not be ignored.

In pursuing this policy, Özal has to reckon with resistance from various directions. First of all, Turkey's most important power factor is the army, which not only sees itself as the guardian of Kemal's legacy, as already mentioned, but also sees itself as the only constant power factor in Turkish domestic politics. Governments of various political hues have come and gone, but the army has remained, and whenever Kemal's legacy appeared threatened in its eyes, it intervened. If Özal succeeds in convincing the Turkish military of the correctness of his course, he will have an easy time of it. For this to happen, however, a very complex process of rethinking must be initiated in the ranks of the military. They have to say goodbye to the attitude of disregard and contempt for international and supranational bodies and their decisions that has been cultivated since Kemal's time. One of the basic principles of Europe is the voluntary surrender of state sovereignty in favour of the community.

The military will also have to say goodbye to the remnants of Great Turkish thinking. Since the end of the Second World War, conflicts in Europe have been solved peacefully through negotiations and not through military pressure. In the future, Turkey's political importance in the region will depend far more on economic factors than on military ones.

Özal's position, however, is facilitated by a process of rethinking towards Europe that has meanwhile begun in the armed forces and is slowly beginning to replace their previous stance of maintaining the status quo.

But it is not only the Turkish military that will have to turn away from traditional patterns of behaviour, but also the diplomatic and political establishment. For the former, the same applies in principle as what has been said for the military, and for the politicians, expansionist policies must no longer be a goal. The conflict with the neighbour must not become an issue of domestic politics.

Another factor that applies equally to Greece and Turkey (much less so to Cyprus) is the strongly personalistic political structure of both countries. The political parties of both countries have clientelistic structures. Decisions are made sovereignly by the heads of the patronage networks, but are also strongly personalised as a result. The advantages of such a system are obvious, as the example of Papandreou and özal shows. However, the process of Greek--Turkish rapprochement thereby depends solely on the will and well-being of two leader personalities, as became clear in connection with Papandreou's decline in power due to illness and private life.

Furthermore, such a political structure naturally opens the door to foreign influence, as the past of both countries has shown. At present, however, this disadvantage could be a blessing for the region. Cleverly applied back-stage diplomacy by the powers interested in conflict resolution could influence both the leaders of Turkey's military and political establishment and Greece's opposition leaders in favour of resolving the conflict. If, for example, the Europeans succeed in convincing Turkish President Evren and, through him, the Turkish military of the usefulness of a peace settlement, the Cyprus conflict could be resolved in the near future, if not within the envisaged timeframe. For Denktash's main support lies with the military in Ankara. If they make him clearly understand that they want the conflict to be resolved, he will give up his intransigent stance, provided, of course, that the Greek Cypriot side helps him find a face-saving solution.

At the meeting of Özal and Papandreou in Athens, both sides apparently came to the conclusion that the Cyprus conflict is easier to solve than the dispute in the Aegean. In view of the process of rethinking in the south of Cyprus in general and in the north among the opposition, this seems plausible. No attempt will be made here to speculate on the details of the future Cyprus settlement, but some essentials can already be noted.

The future Republic of Cyprus will have a new constitution, which will be based on two equal state peoples and create a federal order. The federal state in the north will have a predominantly Turkish character and its southern counterpart a predominantly Greek character. The central government will have the same powers as other federal governments. The legislature will be bicameral with a House of Representatives proportionate to the population and a Senate in which the federal special interests will be safeguarded.

The three freedoms so often propagated will ultimately be guaranteed. In the transitional phase, which must be much shorter than the 18 years propagated by Denktash, they will, however, be subject to certain restrictions in order to prevent possible friction. The proposal of an exchange of property between North and South Cyprus does not seem unreasonable, provided that the exchange takes place on a voluntary basis without forced expropriations. Its impact could also be mitigated by the return of certain previously occupied areas (e.g. Famagousta), where tens of thousands of refugees could find a new home. In terms of foreign policy, the new republic will continue to steer a course of non-alignment.

Without the security guarantee demanded by the Turkish and Turkish Cypriot side, there will be no solution. This problem is exacerbated by Denktash's insistence that the Turkish army take over this guarantee. The Greek Cypriot side, on the other hand, is demanding the withdrawal of the Turkish occupation forces. One conceivable solution, which is being discussed in both Southern and Northern Cyprus, would be to send a European peacekeeping force under UN control, in which a Turkish and a Greek unit would be integrated. In this way, the security needs of both sides would be taken into account and at the same time the face of the respective mother country would be preserved. Provided there is goodwill on both sides and strict discretion, a solution to the Cyprus problem seems quite possible.

Resolving the Aegean conflict is far more difficult. Although both sides have committed themselves to a peaceful solution and initial confidence-building measures have been agreed, there are still no signs of any rapprochement on the actual points of conflict. On the Greek side, the Turkish offers of closer economic cooperation are on the one hand quite positive, but on the other hand a certain scepticism can be observed for two reasons. Greek businessmen are hesitant to become financially involved because they remember the expropriation measures of the 1960s and do not really trust the guarantees offered. On the other hand, there are fears, especially in government circles, that good economic cooperation without prior conflict resolution could lead to the impression in European public opinion that the Greek-Turkish conflict has been resolved. The still unresolved Turkish-Iraqi relations act as a deterrent.

Athens is aware that the bi-lateral conflict is difficult to understand in European public opinion because of its difficult legal nature. It is feared that in the case of closer economic cooperation, the simplistic Turkish PR policy could operate even more successfully than before. At first glance, the solution to the conflict seems quite simple: Ankara would only have to respect international law. However, this would mean _ that Ankara would have to agree to drop its claims in the Aegean. But since all governments since 1 974 have made these claims and influenced Turkish public opinion in this direction, such a solution seems impossible at present.

The Greek position, on the other hand, is largely secured by international and customary international law. If Athens and Ankara were to go together to the International Court of Justice in The Hague, it is very likely that the decision would be in Greece's favour. However, Özal would certainly not be able to survive such a decision in terms of domestic politics. This makes this solution inopportune. Neither Papandreou nor any other Greek prime minister would survive unilateral major concessions from the Greek side politically, not even after winning elections. This solution is therefore also out of the question.

What remains is a compromise solution that saves face for both sides. Unofficially, Athens has been ready for years for a solution according to the Facade Maritime principle and for joint ventures in the Aegean, but its domestic implementation is also likely to be difficult, as it would undoubtedly be branded by the opposition as a betrayal of the national cause. In return, Ankara would have to renounce all claims in the Aegean and, above all, lift the military threat to Greece by disbanding the so-called Aegean Army. Such a move by Ankara could calm Greek public opinion enough for a Greek government to dare to take such a step. At the same time, such a step would move Ankara a long way towards the EC, since in that case Athens would certainly not veto Turkish EC accession.

Consequently, little is likely to happen on the Aegean conflict before the 1989 elections. It is certain that Papandreou's PASOK will fall short of an absolute majority in the elections. Should the election result still be enough for a left majority and the formation of a left coalition government, Papandreou's room for manoeuvre would be severely limited, leaving little room for solo moves, grand gestures or bold steps. If the conservative opposition wins, the process of rapprochement between the two countries will certainly not be broken off, but given the personalistic structure of Greek politics, it is questionable whether reconciliation would be pursued with the same verve and commitment as under Papandreou and Özal, who "can do with each other".

Another consequence of the Greek government's extensive paralysis is an indirect weakening of Vassiliou's position. Although Greek foreign policy will undoubtedly continue to support Vassiliou's efforts to find a solution to the Cyprus problem, it seems questionable whether it will be able to give them the attention they deserve and the diplomatic flank protection they need in view of the domestic situation and the approaching elections. The Cypriot government under Vassiliou will therefore be forced to fight the battle for a solution to the Cyprus problem largely on its own in the coming months. It is to be hoped that the commitment of the Europeans to the Cyprus issue is serious and that this will make up for Athens' failure. use a veto as an alibi to keep Turkey out of the EC. While such a manoeuvre is not yet on the horizon, given the fears of some European countries of an uncontrolled influx of hundreds of thousands of Turkish guest workers, it is not entirely out of the question. Both Athens and Nicosia should not ignore this aspect in their EC policies. It is clear, however, that the EC states can contribute more to the solution of the Cyprus conflict than the Western European public has so far been aware of.

In contrast to the Cyprus conflict, the bilateral Aegean conflict has hardly been "internationalised" or "Europeanised". Neither NATO nor the EC have so far shown any inclination to intervene in this dispute. The Islamic Revolution in Iran (1979), the Soviet invasion of Afghanistan (1979), the Gulf War (1980), the Israeli invasion of Lebanon (1982) caused

Turkey's strategic importance to rise unexpectedly in the eyes of the Reagan administration. External signs of this were the modernisation of the US installations in Turkey (1982) and the constant attempts of the Reagan administration to change the legally anchored 7:10 ratio in favour of Turkey against the will of Congress. In addition, the Turkish generals constantly proved to be compliant allies who also effectively fought Reagan's main enemy, terrorism (communism).

The left-wing PASOK ruling in Athens filled the US administration with deep suspicion, jealously guarding Greek sovereignty and repeatedly threatening to close US bases in the face of real or imagined violations of it. In the eyes of the Reagan administration, these were attempts to humiliate the . USA. It is little wonder, therefore, that the US administration turned a deaf ear to Greek demands for guarantees against an attack from the east, cared little for the legal dispute over the shelf and left the settlement of the Cyprus dispute to the UN Secretary General; knowing full well that he alone would achieve little. This was despite the fact that the US itself had been instrumental in creating the problem in the past. Only recently (after Vassiliou's visit to Washington) has there been a somewhat greater interest on the part of the USA in the Cyprus conflict. But the international conference proposed by Gorbachev is still rejected by Washington (as well as by Ankara). The solution of the Aegean conflict is thus left to Ankara and Athens for the time being.

But it is precisely in bilateral relations that a radical change has taken place, fuelling the hope that the Aegean conflict can also be resolved. For years, both sides avoided dialogue and at best had indirect contacts through NATO channels or via the USA.

The shock of the March crisis of 1987 initiated a process of rethinking. On both sides, the decisive statesmen are in favour of rapprochement. But there are also forces on both sides that are watching the reconciliation process with suspicion, want to maintain the status quo or even continue the traditional course of confrontation.

On the Turkish side, Prime Minister Özal seems determined to end the conflict with Greece. The motives guiding him are of a complex foreign and domestic political nature: one point that receives little attention in the analysis from a European perspective is the desire of Özal and the Turkish military to modernise the country's armed forces. Due to a lack of foreign currency, this can only be done through American and allied military aid. However, American military aid has been fixed by Congress at the 7:10 ratio. The Reagan administration constantly tried to circumvent this regulation, but was regularly prevented from doing so by Congress, due to the influence of the extremely efficient Greek lobby in Congress. A change in the attitude of Congress on this issue can therefore only be expected if özal succeeds in convincing the Greek lobby of his peaceful intentions towards Greece and Cyprus.

On the other hand, Özal fears Islamic fundamentalism (even if he occasionally flirts with the fundamentalists for reasons of coalition arithmetic), which could also overtake Turkey and threaten the secular state created by Kemal Atatürk. This fear is also shared by the Turkish army, which sees itself as the guardian of Kemalism. Özal can therefore count on the support of the military in his defence against fundamentalism.

Özal's concept for warding off the fundamentalist danger is, strictly speaking, the same as Atatürk's. He wants Turkey to become a European country. He wants to turn Turkey into a European country. Özal knows that the EC is more than sceptical about Turkey joining the community. He is also aware that without a prior settlement of the Cyprus conflict and an end to the bilateral Greek-Turkish conflict, the Europeans are not even prepared to start preliminary talks. Before he can normalise relations with Europe, this regional conflict must be resolved.

He knows that in addition to the general European concerns, Athens will veto Turkey's EC accession unless the overall conflict is resolved first. The Turkish side occasionally argues that a solution to the conflict would be easier if Turkey were first admitted to the Community and then the conflict was resolved within the Community. But the intention behind this argumentation is transparent:

Ankara would still try to solve the Aegean conflict in its own interests. The community will be careful not to increase its internal difficulties immeasurably through this conflict. And Athens will hardly be willing to give up its only trump card in the poker game for the resolution of the conflict.

Özal's motives for joining the EC are not limited to the defence against fundamentalism. He and the rest of the Turkish ruling elite, both civilian and military, dream of making Turkey a power factor in the Middle East region, not only in military terms but also in economic and political terms. This long-term goal can also only be achieved with Europe's help.

Another motive is probably the growing difficulties of the Turkish economy, which are exacerbated by the burden of financing the "TRNC"'. Another aspect is Özal's attempt to strengthen the civilian government and prevent future interventions by the army, a policy similar to that of Greece after 1974. The impact of international pressure should also not be ignored.

In pursuing this policy, Özal has to reckon with resistance from various directions. First of all, Turkey's most important power factor is the army, which not only sees itself as the guardian of Kemal's legacy, as already mentioned, but also sees itself as the only constant power factor in Turkish domestic politics. Governments of various political hues have come and gone, but the army has remained, and whenever Kemal's legacy appeared threatened in its eyes, it intervened. If Özal succeeds in convincing the Turkish military of the correctness of his course, he will have an easy time of it. For this to happen, however, a very complex process of rethinking must be initiated in the ranks of the military. They have to say goodbye to the attitude of disregard and contempt for international and supranational bodies and their decisions that has been cultivated since Kemal's time. One of the basic principles of Europe is the voluntary surrender of state sovereignty in favour of the community.

The military will also have to say goodbye to the remnants of great Turkish thinking. Since the end of the Second World War, conflicts in Europe have been resolved peacefully through negotiations and not through military pressure. In the future, Turkey's political importance in the region will depend far more on economic factors than on military ones.

Özal's position is, however, facilitated by a process of rethinking towards Europe that has meanwhile begun in the armed forces and is slowly beginning to replace their previous stance of maintaining the status quo.

But it is not only the Turkish military that will have to turn away from traditional patterns of behaviour, but also the diplomatic and political establishment. For the former, the same applies in principle as what has been said for the military, and for the politicians, expansionist policies must no longer be a target. The conflict with the neighbour must not become an issue of domestic politics.

Another factor that applies equally to Greece and Turkey (much less so to Cyprus) is the strongly personalistic political structure of both countries. The political parties of both countries have clientelistic structures. Decisions are made sovereignly by the heads of the patronage networks, but are also strongly personalised as a result. The advantages of such a system are obvious, as the example of Papandreou and Özal shows. However, the process of Greek-Turkish rapprochement thereby depends solely on the will and well-being of two leader personalities, as became clear in connection with Papandreou's decline in power due to illness and private life.

Furthermore, such a political structure naturally opens the door to foreign influence, as the past of both countries has shown. At present, however, this disadvantage could be a blessing for the region. Cleverly applied back-stage diplomacy by the powers interested in conflict resolution could influence both the leaders of Turkey's military and political establishment and Greece's opposition leaders in favour of resolving the conflict. If, for example, the Europeans succeed in convincing Turkish President ,Evren, and through him the Turkish military, of the usefulness of a peace settlement, the Cyprus conflict could be solved, if not within the envisaged period, then at least in the near future. For Denktash's main support lies with the military in Ankara. If they make him clearly understand that they want the conflict to be resolved, he will give up his intransigent stance, provided, of course, that the Greek Cypriot side helps him find a face-saving solution.

At the meeting of Özal and Papandreou in Athens, both sides apparently came to the conclusion that the Cyprus conflict is easier to solve than the dispute in the Aegean. In view of the rethinking process in the south of Cyprus in general and in the north among the opposition, this seems plausible. No attempt will be made here to speculate on the details of the future Cyprus settlement, but some essentials can already be noted.

The future Republic of Cyprus will have a new constitution, which will be based on two equal state peoples and create a federal state order. The federal state in the north will have a predominantly Turkish character and its southern counterpart a predominantly Greek one. The central government will have the same powers as other federal governments. The legislature will be bicameral with a House of Representatives proportionate to the population and a Senate in which the federal special interests will be safeguarded.

The three freedoms so often propagated will ultimately be guaranteed. In the transitional phase, which must be much shorter than the 1 8 years propagated by Denktash, they will, however, be subject to certain restrictions in order to prevent possible friction. The proposal of an exchange of property between North and South Cyprus does not seem outlandish, provided that the exchange is voluntary and does not involve compulsory expropriation. Its impact could also be mitigated by the return of certain previously occupied areas (e.g. Famagousta), where tens of thousands of refugees could find a new home. In terms of foreign policy, the new republic will continue to steer a course of non-alignment.

Without the security guarantee demanded by the Turkish and Turkish Cypriot side, there will be no solution. This problem is exacerbated by Denktash's insistence that the Turkish army take over this guarantee. The Greek Cypriot side, on the other hand, is demanding the withdrawal of the Turkish occupation forces. One conceivable solution, which is being discussed in both southern and northern Cyprus, would be to send a European peacekeeping force under UN control, in which a Turkish and a Greek unit would be integrated. In this way, the security needs of both sides would be taken into account and at the same time the face of the respective mother country would be preserved. Provided there is goodwill on both sides and strict discretion, a solution to the Cyprus problem seems quite possible.

Resolving the Aegean conflict is far more difficult. Although both sides have committed themselves to a peaceful solution and initial confidence-building measures have been agreed, there are still no signs of any rapprochement on the actual points of conflict. On the Greek side, the Turkish offers of closer economic cooperation are on the one hand quite positive, but on the other hand a certain scepticism can be observed for two reasons. Greek businessmen are hesitant to become financially involved because they remember the expropriation measures of the 1960s and do not really trust the guarantees offered. On the other hand, there are fears, especially in government circles, that good economic cooperation without prior conflict resolution could lead to the impression in European public opinion that the Greek-Turkish conflict has been resolved. The still unresolved Turkish-Iraqi relations act as a deterrent.

Athens is aware that the bi-lateral conflict is difficult to understand in European public opinion because of its difficult legal nature. It is feared that in the case of closer economic cooperation, the simplistic Turkish PR policy could operate even more successfully than before. At first glance, the solution to the conflict seems quite simple: Ankara would only have to respect international law. However, this would mean that Ankara would have to drop its claims in the Aegean. But since all governments since 1974 have made these claims and influenced Turkish public opinion in this direction, such a solution seems impossible at present.

The Greek position, on the other hand, is largely secured by international and customary international law. If Athens and Ankara were to go together to the International Court of Justice in The Hague, it is very likely that the decision would be in Greece's favour. However, Özal would certainly not be able to survive such a decision in terms of domestic politics. This makes this solution inopportune. Neither Papandreou nor any other Greek prime minister would survive unilateral major concessions from the Greek side politically, not even after winning elections. This solution is therefore also out of the question.

What remains is a compromise solution that saves face for both sides. Unofficially, Athens has been prepared for years to accept a solution based on the Facade Maritime principle and joint ventures in the Aegean, but this would also be difficult to implement domestically, as it would undoubtedly be branded by the opposition as a betrayal of the national cause. In return, Ankara would have to renounce all claims in the Aegean and, above all, lift the military threat to Greece by disbanding the so-called Aegean Army. Such a move by Ankara could calm Greek public opinion enough for a Greek government to dare to take such a step. At the same time, such a step would move Ankara a long way towards the EC, since in that case Athens would certainly not veto Turkish EC accession.

However, in view of the permanent crisis in Athens, such a solution seems extremely unlikely at present. Before the crisis, it would have been conceivable against the background of a renewed electoral victory by Papandreou due to a prior resolution of the Cyprus conflict that would have brought about a total turnaround in Greek public opinion. However, based on the current domestic political situation, such a development is hardly conceivable.

Consequently, little is likely to happen on the Aegean conflict before the 1989 elections. It is certain that Papandreou's PASOK will fall short of an absolute majority in the elections. Should the election result still be enough for a left majority and the formation of a left coalition government, Papandreou's room for manoeuvre would be severely limited, leaving little room for solo moves, grand gestures or bold steps. If the conservative opposition wins, the process of rapprochement between the two countries will certainly not be broken off, but given the personalistic structure of Greek politics, it is questionable whether reconciliation would be pursued with the same verve and commitment as under Papandreou and Özal, who "can do with each other".

Another consequence of the Greek government's paralysis is the indirect weakening of Vassiliou's position. Although Greek foreign policy will undoubtedly continue to support Vassiliou's efforts to find a solution to the Cyprus problem, it seems questionable whether, in view of the domestic situation and the approaching elections, it will be able to give them the attention they deserve and provide the diplomatic flank protection they need. The Cypriot government under Vassiliou will therefore be forced to fight the battle for a solution to the Cyprus problem largely on its own in the coming months. It is to be hoped that the commitment of the Europeans to the Cyprus problem is serious and that this will make up for the failure of Athens.

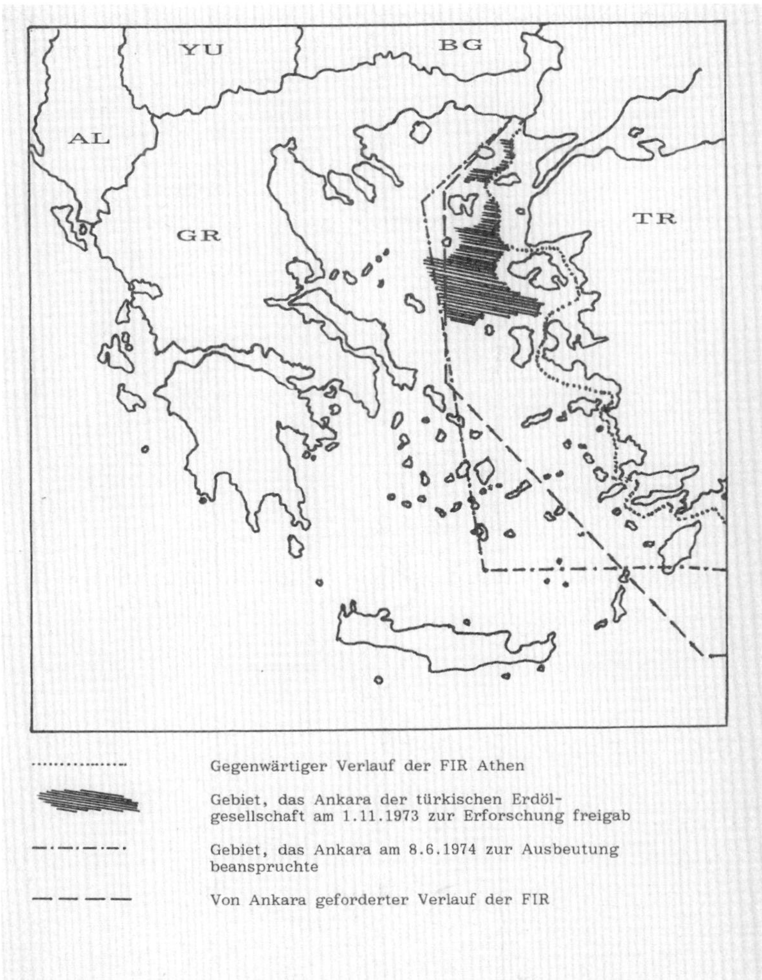

...... - Present course of the FIR Athens
- Area released for exploration by the Turkish Petroleum Company on 1. 11. 1973.
- Area. which Ankara claimed for exploitation on 8. 6.1974
- From Ankara demanded route of the FIR

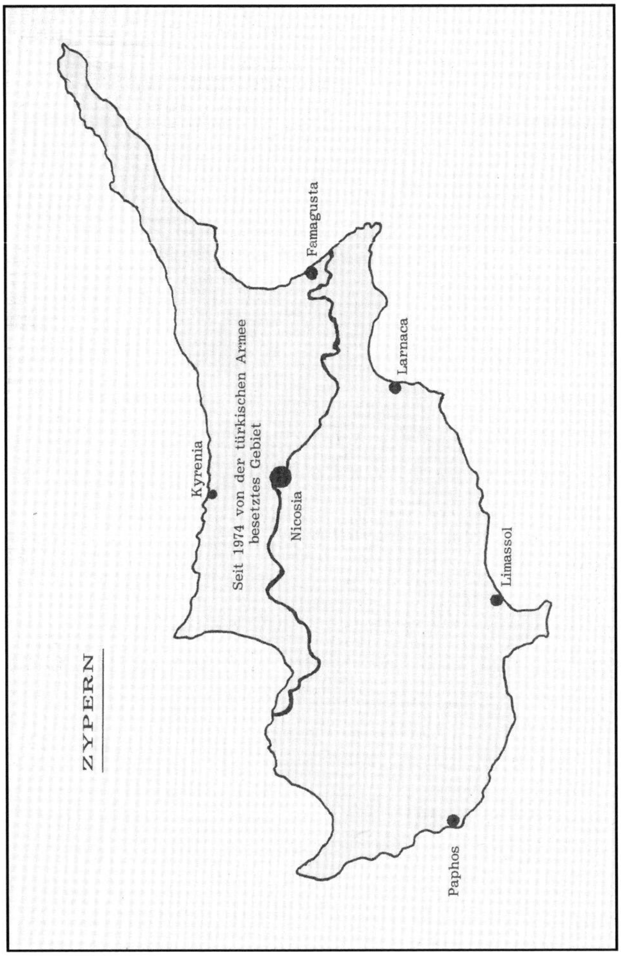
ZYPERN
Kyrenia
Seit 1974 von der türkischen Armee besetztes Gebiet
Nicosia
Famagusta
Larnaca
Limassol
Paphos

SELECT BIBLIOGRAPHY

Bibliographies

Coufoudakis, Van "A Bibliography on Greek -Turkish Relations", *Modern Greek Society: A Social Science Newsletter,* 13:1 (1985), pp .5-60

Kitromilidis, Paschalis; Evriviadis, Marios, *Cyprus.* (Oxford: Clio Press, 1982)

Richter, Heinz A.
Greece and Cyprus since 1920. Bibliography of Contemporary History. (Heidelberg: Nea Hellas, 1984)

Zenelis, John G.
United States Policy Toward Greece and Cyprus Since the Second World War. A Bibliography. (New York: Pella, 1980)

Specialized Literature

Adams, Thomas; Cotrell, Alvin,
Cyprus between East and West. (Baltimore: 1968)

Alexandris, Alexis,
The Greek Minority of Istanbul and Greek-Turkish Relations 1918-1974. (Athens: 1983)

Analis, Dimitri,
Chypre, Operation Attila. (Paris: Editions Anthropos, 1978)

Attalides, Michael,
Cyprus. Nationalism and International Politics (Edinburg: 1979)

idem. (ed.),
Cyprus Reviewed (Nikosia: Zavallis, 1977)

Barkman, C. D.,
Ambassadeur in Athene. 1969-1975 *van Dictatuur tot Demokratie.* (Gravenhage 1984)

Coufoudakis, Van,
United States Foreign Policy, in: *US Foreign Policy toward* Greece and Cyprus. The Clash of Principle and Pragmatism. Edited by Theodore A. Couloumbis u. Sallie M. Hicks, (Washington, 1975)

Couloumbis, Theodore A.,
The United States, Greece, and Turkey. The Troubled Triangle. (New York: 1983)

Couloumbis, T. A.; Petropoulos, J. A.; Psomiades, H. J. (eds.),
Foreign Interference in Greek Politics: A Historical Perspective. (New York: Pella, 1976)

Crouzet, Francois,
Le conflict de Chypre 1946-1959. Vol I. (Bruxelles, 1973)

Dabag, Mihran; Sen, Faruk; Yiallouridis, Christodoulos,
Der griechisch-türkisch-zypriotische Konflikt als internationaler Modellkonflikt. Bestandsaufnahme und Lösungsstrategien anhand empirischer Untersuchungen gesellschaftlicher Subsysteme. (Athen. Bochum. Bonn. 1986)

Dean, Philip,
I Should Have Died. (London: 1976)

Dischler, Ludwig,
Die Zypernfrage (Frankfurt: Metzner, 1960)

Eden, Anthony,
Full Circle. (London: 1960)
Eren, Eren,
"Die türkisch-sowjetischen Beziehungen", *Europa Archiv, 9,* (1965), p. 337
Ertekün, Necati,
The Cyprus Dispute and the Birth of the Turkish Republic of Northern Cyprus. (Nicosia: Rustem, 1981)
Faulds, Andrew (ed.),
Excerpta Cypria for Today. A Source Book on the Cyprus Problem. (Nicosia: Rustem, 1988)
Fernau, Friedrich-Wilhelm,
"Nachbarschaft am Schwarzen Meer", *Europa Archiv,* 17, (1967), p. 616
Feyzioglu, Turhan,
Chypre. Mythes et Realites. Documents sur le Probleme de Chypre. (Ankara: Institut de Politique Etrangere, 1984)
Foley, Charles,
Legacy of Strife: Cyprus from Rebellion to CMI War. (Harmondsworth: Penguin, 1964)
Guisan, Isabelle,
"Die letzten Byzantiner gehen in aller Stille unter", *Pogrom,* Nr. 123, (1986), p. 46ff
Harbottle, Michael,
The Impartial Soldier. (London: Oxford University Press, 1970)
Hitchens, Christopher,
Cyprus (London: Quartet Books, 1984)
Kadritzke, Niels; Wagner, Wolf,
Im Fadenkreuz der Nato. Ermittlungen am Beispiel Cypern.
(Berlin: Rotbuch Verlag, 1976)
Karaosmanoglu, Ali L.,
"Turkey's Security and the Middle East" *Foreign Affairs,* 62:1(1983), p. 158
Koufoudakis [Coufoudakis], Vangelis [Van],
I Kypros kai oi yperdynameis *1960* -1979, in: G.Tenekidis and G. Kranidiotis (eds.) *Kypros. Istoria. provlimata kai agones tou laou tis.* (Athens, 1981), p 372
Koumoulides, John T. A. (ed.),
Cyprus in Transition 1960 -1985. (London: Trigraph, 1986)
Kuniholm, Bruce,
The Origins of the Cold War in the Near East. Great Power Conflict and Diplomacy in Iran, Turkey and Greece. (Princeton: Princeton University Press, 1980)
Kyriakidis, Stanley,
Cyprus Constitutionalism and Crisis Government. (Philadelphia: Pennsylvania University Press, 1968)
Ladas, S. P.,
The Exchange of Minorities: Bulgaria, Greece and Turkey. (New York: 1932)

Landau, Jacob M.,
"Johnson's 1964 Letter to Inönü and Greek Lobbying of the White House", in: *Jerusalem Papers on Peace Problems* (Jerusalem: The Leonard Davis Institute for International Relations, 1979), pp. 19-22

Meinardus, Ronald,
"Eine neue Phase im Zypern-Konflikt", *Europa-Archiv,* Folge 10, (1984), p. 299

idem *Die Türkei-Politik Griechenlands* (Frankfurt: Peter Lang, 1985)

Mühleisen, Hans-Otto,
"Der Zypernkonflikt 1950-1984", in: Johst Dülffer; Hans-Otto Mühleisen; Vera Torunsky, *Inseln als Brennpunkte internationaler Politik. Konfliktbewältigung im Wandel des internationalen Systems 1890-1984: Kreta, Korfu, Zypern.*(Köln: Berend von Nottbeck, 1986), pp. 97-144

Nejatigil, Z. M.,
Our Republic in Perspective. (Nicosia: 1985)

Ökte, Faik,
The Tragedy of the Turkish Capital Tax (London: Croom Helm, 1987)

Pallis, A. A.,
Greece's Anatolian Venture and After. (London: 1937)

Papandreou, Andreas,
Democracy at Gunpoint: The Greek Front. (New York: 1970)

Pentzopoulos, D.,
The Balkan Exchange of Minorities and its Impact upon Greece. (The Hague: 1962)

Polyviou, Polyvios G.,
Cyprus. Conflict and Negotiation 1960 -1980. (London: Duckworth, 1980)

Purcell, H.,
Cyprus. (London: 1969)

Reddaway, John,
Burdened with Cyprus. The British Connection. (Nicosia: Austern, 1986)

Sauerwein, Friedrich,
Spannungsfeld Ägäis. Informationen, Hintergründe, Ursachen des griechisch-türkischen Konflikts um Zypern und die Ägäis. (Frankfurt: Diesterweg, 1980)

Stavrou, N. A.,
Allied Politics and Military Interventions: The Political Role of the Greek Military. (Athen: Papazisis, 1977)

Steinbach, Udo,
"Neuere Entwicklungen in den politischen Beziehungen zwischen der Sowjetunion und der Türkei, Griechenland und Zypern", *Osteuropa,* (1973), p. 532

Stern, Laurence,
"Bitter Lessons: How we Failed in Cyprus", *Foreign Policy,* (Summer 1974)

Tsouderos, Emmanouil,
Diplomatika paraskinia 1941 -1944 (Athen: Aetos, 1950)

Tsoucalas, Constantine,
The Greek Tragedy. (Harmondsworth: Penguin, 1969)

Weber, Frank,
The Evasive Neutral. Germany, Britain and the Quest for a Turkish Alliance in the Second World War. (London: 1979)

Wilson, Andrew,

The Aegean Dispute. (London: 1979)

Woodhouse, C. M.,

Apple of Discord. A Survey of Recent Greek Politics in Their International Setting (London: Hutchinson, 1948)

Xydis, Stephen,

Cyprus: Conflict and Conciliation, 1954-1958. (Columbus, Ohio: Ohio State University Press, 1967)

Idem

Cyprus, Reluctant Republic. (The Hague: Mouton, 1973)

In the meantime the author published the following studies on the Cyprus conflict in the PELEUS series, which had appeared earlier in German:

Heinz A. Richter *Cyprus in the 19th and 20th Century. Collected articles*
Peleus No. 108 (2021)

idem *History of the Island of Cyprus 1878-1977.* 4 vols.
Peleus Nos 109-112 (2021)

idem *The Greek-Turkish War 1919-1922.* (2016) Peleus 73

The Peleus series is published by Harrassowitz in Wiesbaden, Germany.

Additional Peleus titles in German and English can be founde here:
www.rutzen-verlag.de

Band 112 **Heinz A. Richter, History of the Island of Cyprus. Part 4: 1965–1977**. 766 pages, hc, 80,- Euro, ISBN 978-3-447-11734-0

Band 111 **Heinz A. Richter, History of the Island of Cyprus. Part 3: 1959–1965**. 524 pages, hc, 60,- Euro, ISBN 978-3-447-11695-4

Band 110 **Heinz A. Richter, History of the Island of Cyprus. Part 2: 1950–1959**. 534 pages, hc, 60,- Euro, ISBN 978-3-447-11659-6

Band 109 **Heinz A. Richter, History of the Island of Cyprus. Part 1: 1878–1949**. 436 pages, hc, 60,- Euro, ISBN 978-3-447-11643-5

Band 108 **Heinz A. Richter, Cyprus in the 19th & 20th Century**. 180 pages, hc, 30,- Euro, ISBN 978-3-447-11629-9

Band 107 **Heinz A. Richter, Greece in the 20th Century**. 208 pages, hc, 30,- Euro, ISBN 978-3-447-11627-5

Band 106 **Heinz A. Richter, The Turkish Straits in International Politics 1900–1917**. 270 pages, hc, 40,- Euro, ISBN 978-3-447-11591-9

Band 105 **Heinz A. Richter, Greek Military Lines of Defence 1941**. 94 pages, hc, 35,- Euro, ISBN 978-3-447-11589-6

Band 104 **Heinz A. Richter, History of the Cypriot Left**. 218 pages, hc, 35,- Euro, ISBN 978-3-447-11566-7

Band 103,2 **Heinz A. Richter, History of Greece in the 20th Century**. 442 pages, hc, 49,- Euro, ISBN 978-3-447-11539-1

Band 103,1 **Heinz A. Richter, History of Greece in the 20th Century**. 320 pages, hc, 40,- Euro, ISBN 978-3-447-11538-4

Band 102 **Heinz A. Richter, History of the Greek Left**. 526 pages, hc, 59,- Euro, ISBN 978-3-447-11526-1

Band 101 **Heinz A. Richter, Greece 1950–1974**. 528 pages, hc, 59,- Euro, ISBN 978-3-447-11502-5

Band 99 **Heinz A. Richter, Greece 1940-1950**. 400 pages, hc, 49,- Euro, ISBN 978-3-447-11455-4

Band 98 **Eckhard Lisec, Turkish Armed Forces**. 154 pages, hc, 30,- Euro, ISBN 978-3-447-11438-7

Band 97 **Heinz A. Richter, Greece in World War II. 1939–1941**. 422 pages, hc, 45,- Euro, ISBN 978-3-447-11436-3

Band 96 **Heinz A. Richter, Macedonia 1915–1918**. 190 pages, hc, 39,- Euro, ISBN 978-3-447-11422-6

Band 95 **Heinz A. Richter, Gallipoli 1915**. 270 pages, hc, 45,- Euro, ISBN 978-3-447-11393-9

Band 94 **Heinz A. Richter, Griechische Verteidigungslinien 1941. Die Metaxas-Linie**. 100 Seiten, gb, 30,- Euro, ISBN 978-3-447-11378-6

Band 93 **Heinz A. Richter, Operation Mercury**. 308 pages, hc, 45,- Euro, ISBN 978-3-447-11323-6

Band 92 **Heinz A. Richter, Greece 1947–1967**. 120 pages, hc, 30,- Euro, ISBN 978-3-447-11255-0

Band 91 **Heinz A. Richter, Greece 1936–1946**. 192 pages, hc, 35,- Euro, ISBN 978-3-447-11241-3

Band 90 **Heinz A. Richter, German-Greek Relations 1940–1960**. 108 pages, hc, 30,- Euro, ISBN 978-3-447-11177-5

Band 89 **Heinz A. Richter, Modern Greek Myths**. 104 pages, hc, 19,80 Euro, ISBN 978-3-447-11165-2

Band 88 **Heinz A. Richter, Aspekte neugriechischer Geschichte**. 132 Seiten, gb, 30,- Euro, ISBN 978-3-447-11132-4

Band 87 **Heinz A. Richter, The Greeks in the Ottoman Empire 1913–1923**. 188 pages, 32 plates, 74 photos, 4 maps, 40,- Euro, ISBN 978-3-447-11150-8

Band 86 **Heinz A. Richter, Die Griechen im Osmanischen Reich 1913–1923**. 198 Seiten, gb, 40,- Euro, ISBN 978-3-447-11131-7

Band 85 **Heinz A. Richter, The Ottoman Empire in World War I until the peace in 1923**. 222 pages, hc, 40,- Euro, ISBN 978-3-447-11045-7

Band 84 **Heinz A. Richter, Das Osmanische Reich im Ersten Weltkrieg bis zum Friedenschluss 1923**. 242 Seiten, gb, 40,- Euro, ISBN 978-3-447-11038-9

Band 80 **Heinz A. Richter, Die türkischen Meerengen in der internationalen Politik 1900–1917**. 274 Seiten, gb, 40,- Euro, ISBN 978-3-447-10915-4

Band 79 **Heinz A. Richter, Geschichte der zypriotischen Linken**. 254 Seiten, gb, 30,- Euro, ISBN 978-3-447-10867-6

Band 78 **Harald Gilbert, Der Krieg in der Ägäis 1943–1944**. 332 Seiten, gb, 40,- Euro, ISBN 978-3-447-10913-0

Band 77 **Heinz A. Richter, Geschichte der griechischen Linken**. 558 Seiten, gb, 50,- Euro, ISBN 978-3-447-10846-1

Band 76 **Heinz A. Richter, Hellas und Zypern in meinem Leben**. 179 Seiten, gb, 30,- Euro, ISBN 978-3-447-10769-3

Band 74	**Heinz A. Richter, Mythen und Legenden in der griechischen Zeitgeschichte.** 116 Seiten, gb, 19,80 Euro, ISBN 978-3-447-10703-7
Band 73	**Heinz A. Richter, The Greek-Turkish War 1919–1922.** 211 pages, hc, 30,- Euro, ISBN 978-3-447-10671-9
Band 72	**Heinz A. Richter, Griechisch-türkischer Krieg 1919–22.** 222 Seiten, gb, 30,- Euro, ISBN 978-3-447-10656-6
Band 71	**Johannes Fouquet, Lydia Gaitanou (Hg.), Im Schatten der Alten?** 193 Seiten, gb, 40,- Euro, ISBN 978-3-447-10450-0
Band 70	**Heinz A. Richter (Hg.), Griechenland 1942–43.** 320 Seiten, gb, 28,- Euro, ISBN 978-3-447-10460-9
Band 69	**Heinz A. Richter, Griechenland 1945–1946.** 456 Seiten, gb, 49,- Euro, ISBN 978-3-447-10533-0
Band 68	**Heinz A. Richter, Griechenland 1915–1917 im Spiegel russischer Akten.** 118 Seiten, gb, 28,- Euro, ISBN 978-3-447-10612-2
Band 67,2	**Heinz A. Richter, Geschichte Griechenlands im 20. Jahrhundert.** 480 Seiten, gb, 49,- Euro, ISBN 978-3-447-10398-5
Band 67,1	**Heinz A. Richter, Die Geschichte Griechenlands im 20. Jahrhundert.** 360 Seiten, gb, 40,- Euro, ISBN 978-3-447-10396-1
Band 66,1	**Heinz A. Richter, Reinhard Stupperich (Hg.), Von Mainz nach Kreta im Winter 1942–43.** 128 Seiten, gb, 32,- Euro, ISBN 978-3-447-10304-6
Band 65,2	**Heinz A. Richter, Der Krieg im Südosten: Band 2: Makedonien 1915–1918.** 207 Seiten, gb, 35,- Euro, ISBN 978-3-447-10249-0
Band 65,1	**Heinz A. Richter, Der Krieg im Südosten: Band 1: Gallipoli 1915.** 294 Seiten, gb, 42,- Euro, ISBN 978-3-447-10118-9
Band 64	**Harry Cliadakis, Fascism in Greece.** 152 pages, hc, 32,- Euro, ISBN 978-3-447-10188-2
Band 63	**Harald Gilbert, Das besetzte Kreta. 1941–1945.** 404 Seiten, gb, 49,- Euro, ISBN 978-3-447-10186-8
Band 62	**Joachim Franz, Rosmarie Günther, Reinhard Stupperich (Hg.), „Ein Wald von Statuen“.** 300 Seiten, gb, 37,- Euro, ISBN 978-3-447-10302-2
Band 61	**Mihailo St. Popović, Historische Geographie und Digital Humanities.** 221 Seiten, gb, 32,- Euro, ISBN 978-3-447-06950-2
Band 60	**Heinz A. Richter, Griechenland 1950–1974.** 549 Seiten, gb, 49,- Euro, ISBN 978-3-447-06908-3
Band 59	**Heinz A. Richter, Griechenland 1940–1950.** 484 Seiten, gb, 49,- Euro, ISBN 978-3-447-06704-1
Band 58	**Thorsten Kruse, Bonn – Nikosia – Ostberlin. Innerdeutsche Fehden auf fremden Boden 1960–1972.** 399 Seiten, gb, 49,- Euro, ISBN 978-3-447-06766-9
Band 57	**Ekrem Akurgal, Erinnerungen eines Archäologen.** 224 Seiten, gb, 35,- Euro, ISBN 978-3-447-06875-8
Band 56	**Alexander Papageorgiou-Venetas, In Focus: Athens. Im Brennpunkt: Athen.** 232 Seiten, gb, 44,- Euro, ISBN 978-3-447-06721-8
Band 55	**John Sakkas, Britain and the Greek Civil War 1944–1949.** 159 pages, hc, 30,- Euro, ISBN 978-3-447-06718-8
Band 54	**Heinz A. Richter, Operation Merkur.** 319 Seiten, gb, 49,- Euro, ISBN 978-3-447-06423-1
Band 53	**G. R. Wright, Cypriot Connections.** 214 pages, hc, 39,90 Euro, ISBN 978-3-447-06301-2
Band 52	**Gerhard Weber, Hellmuth Felmy. Stationen einer militärischen Karriere.** 341 Seiten, gb, 45,- Euro, ISBN 978-3-447-06299-2
Band 51	**Maria Deoudi, Die thrakische Jägerin.** 202 Seiten, gb, 35,- Euro, ISBN 978-3-447-06213-8
Band 50	**Heinz A. Richter, A Concise History of Modern Cyprus 1878–2009.** 287 pages, hc, 35,- Euro, ISBN 978-3-447-06212-1
Band 49	**Heinz A. Richter, Kurze Geschichte des modernen Zypern 1878–2009.** 330 Seiten, gb, 35,- Euro, ISBN 978-3-447-06211-4
Band 48	**Lucie Bonato, Maryse Emery, Louis Dumesnil de Maricourt.** 308 pages, relié, 35,- Euro, ISBN 978-3-447-06128-5
Band 47	**Mustafa Bulba, Geometrische Keramik Kariens.** 282 Seiten, gb, 35,- Euro, ISBN 978-3-447-06132-2
Band 46	**Hans-Martin Kirchner, Friedrich Thiersch.** 286 Seiten, gb, 35,- Euro, ISBN 978-3-447-06123-0
Band 45	**Mihailo St. Popović, Mara Branković.** 254 Seiten, gb, 32,- Euro, ISBN 978-3-447-06124-7
Band 44	**Alfons Kitzinger, Ohne Schwert und Kugeln.** 140 Seiten, gb, 32,- Euro, ISBN 978-3-447-05941-1

Band 43 **Glafkos Clerides, Negotiating for Cyprus 1993–2003**. 170 pages, hc, 30,- Euro, ISBN 978-3-447-05989-3

Band 42 **Wolfgang Decker, Die Wiederbelebung der Olympischen Spiele**. 202 Seiten, gb, 30,- Euro, ISBN 978-3-447-05988-6

Band 41 **Heinz A. Richter, Geschichte der Insel Zypern**. 808 Seiten, gb, 65,- Euro, ISBN 978-3-447-05943-5

Band 39 **Vaïos Kalogrias, Okkupation, Widerstand und Kollaboration in Makedonien 1941–1944**. 383 Seiten, gb, 42,- Euro, ISBN 978-3-447-05985-5

Band 38 **Tim Potier, A Functional Cyprus Settlement: the Constitutional Dimension**. 764 pages, hc, 49,- Euro, ISBN 978-3-447-05984-8

Band 37 **Heinz A. Richter, Geschichte der Insel Zypern**. 644 Seiten, gb, 49,- Euro, ISBN 978-3-447-05983-1

Band 36 **Ina E. Minner, Ewig ein Fremder im fremden Lande**. 436 Seiten, gb, 42,50 Euro, ISBN 978-3-447-05982-4

Band 35 **Heinz A. Richter, Geschichte der Insel Zypern**. 665 Seiten, gb, 49,- Euro, ISBN 978-3-447-05981-7

Band 34 **Sozos-Christos Theodoulou, Bases militaires en droit international: le cas de Chypre**. 148 pages, relié, 28,- Euro, ISBN 978-3-447-05980-0

Band 33 **Alexander Jossifidis, Die slawophonen Griechen Makedoniens**. 290 Seiten, gb, 38,- Euro, ISBN 978-3-447-05979-4

Band 32 **Makarios Drousiotis, Cyprus 1974**. 278 pages, hc, 38,- Euro, ISBN 978-3-447-05978-7

Band 30 **Moshe Ha-Elion, The Straits of Hell**. 120 pages, hc, 21,50 Euro, ISBN 978-3-447-05976-3

Band 29 **Heinz A. Richter, Geschichte der Insel Zypern**. 498 Seiten, gb, 42,50 Euro, ISBN 978-3-447-05975-6

Band 28 **Reinhard Stupperich (Hg.), Nova Graecia**. 258 Seiten, gb, 32,- Euro, ISBN 978-3-447-05974-9

Band 27 **James Ker-Lindsay, Britain and the Cyprus Crisis 1963–1964**. 143 pages, hc, 24,50 Euro, ISBN 978-3-447-05973-2

Band 26 **Peter Loizos, The Greek Gift**. 326 pages, hc, 36,50 Euro, ISBN 978-3-447-05972-5

Band 24 **Nicolas D. Macris (Ed.), The 1960 Treaties on Cyprus and Selected Subsequent Acts**. 212 pages, hc, 32,50 Euro, ISBN 978-3-447-05971-8

Band 23 **Elena Pogiatzi, Die Grabreliefs auf Zypern von der archaischen bis zur römischen Zeit**. 307 Seiten, gb, 44,50 Euro, ISBN 978-3-447-05970-1

Band 22 **Vassilis K. Fouskas, Heinz A. Richter (Eds.), Cyprus and Europe**. 212 pages, hc, 32,50 Euro, ISBN 978-3-447-05969-5

Band 21 **Alexander Papageorgiou-Venetas, Städte und Landschaften in Griechenland zur Zeit König Ottos 1833–1862**. 280 Seiten, gb, 49,- Euro, ISBN 978-3-447-05968-8

Band 19 **Hubert Faustmann, Nicos Peristianis (Eds.), Britain in Cyprus**. 660 pages, hc, 49,- Euro, ISBN 978-3-447-05966-4

Band 18 **Michael A. Attalides, Cyprus**. 226 pages, hc, 35,- Euro, ISBN 978-3-447-05965-7

Band 16 **Emanuel Turczynski, Sozial- und Kulturgeschichte Griechenlands im 19. Jahrhundert**. 586 Seiten, gb, 49,50 Euro, ISBN 978-3-447-05964-0

Band 15 **Ioanna Spiliopoulou-Donderer, Kaiserzeitliche Grabaltäre Niedermakedoniens**. 338 Seiten, gb, 37,50 Euro, ISBN 978-3-447-05963-3

Band 14 **John Charalambous, Alicia Chrysostomou, Denis Judd, Heinz A. Richter, Reinhard Stupperich (Eds.), Cyprus: 40 Years on from Independence**. 199 pages, hc, 29,- Euro, ISBN 978-3-447-05962-6

Band 13 **Andreas Stergiou, Im Spagat zwischen Solidarität und Realpolitik**. 199 Seiten, gb, 32,70 Euro, ISBN 978-3-447-05961-9

Band 12 **Hermann Frank Meyer, Von Wien nach Kalavryta**. 556 Seiten, gb, 49,- Euro, ISBN 978-3-447-05960-2

Band 11 **Alexander Papageorgiou-Venetas, Eduard Schaubert 1804–1860**. 192 Seiten, gb, 39,90 Euro, ISBN 978-3-447-05959-6

Band 10 **Ingeborg Huber, Die Ikonographie der Trauer in der Griechischen Kunst**. 271 Seiten, gb, 34,80 Euro, ISBN 978-3-447-05958-9

Band 9 **Claude Nicolet, United States Policy Towards Cyprus 1954–1974**. 483 pages, hc, 42,90 Euro, ISBN 978-3-447-05957-2

Band 8	**Karl Giebeler, Heinz A. Richter, Reinhard Stupperich (Hg.)**, **Versöhnung ohne Wahrheit?** 98 Seiten, gb, 19,90 Euro, ISBN 978-3-447-05956-5
Band 7	**Özdemir A. Özgür**, **Cyprus in My Life**. 174 pages, hc, 24,50 Euro, ISBN 978-3-447-05955-8
Band 6	**Michael Wedde**, **Towards a Hermeneutics of Aegean Bronze Age Ship Imagery**. 356 pages, hc, 46,- Euro, ISBN 978-3-447-05954-1
Band 5	**Joachim G. Joachim**, **Ioannis Metaxas**. 367 pages, hc, 32,20 Euro, ISBN 978-3-447-05953-4
Band 4	**Evangelos Chrysos, Dimitrios Letsios, Heinz A. Richter, Reinhard Stupperich (Hg.)**, **Griechenland und das Meer**. 222 Seiten, gb, 24,50 Euro, ISBN 978-3-447-05952-7
Band 3	**Volker Heenes**, **Die Vasen der Sammlung des Grafen Franz I. von Erbach zu Erbach**. 131 Seiten, br, 25,50 Euro, ISBN 978-3-447-05951-0
Band 2	**Heinz A. Richter**, **Griechenland im Zweiten Weltkrieg 1939–1941**. 456 Seiten, br, 49,- Euro, ISBN 978-3-447-06410-1
Band 1	**Ingrid Krauskopf**, **Heroen, Götter und Dämonen auf etruskischen Skarabäen**. 146 Seiten, br, 14,90 Euro, ISBN 978-3-447-05950-3